CONTENTS

WOULD YOU CHOOSE

TO HAVE AN ELEPHANT'S TRUNK, GET CAUGHT IN A SWARM OF BEES OR SQUIRT YOUR OWN BLOOD AT AN ATTACKER?

Animals and plants of the world have some wicked features to help them survive. In *Wicked Wildlife* you're invited, just for fun, to experience some contrasting wildlife encounters, and choose the wickedest animal features.

Read each question, CONSIDER YOUR OPTIONS, check out the facts,

see what your friends think (and what we chose) and then make YOUR choice.

WHAT WOULD **YOU** CHOOSE?

WICKED **WILDLIFE**

HELEN GREATHEAD

EDGE FRANKLIN WATTS

LONDON·SYDNEY

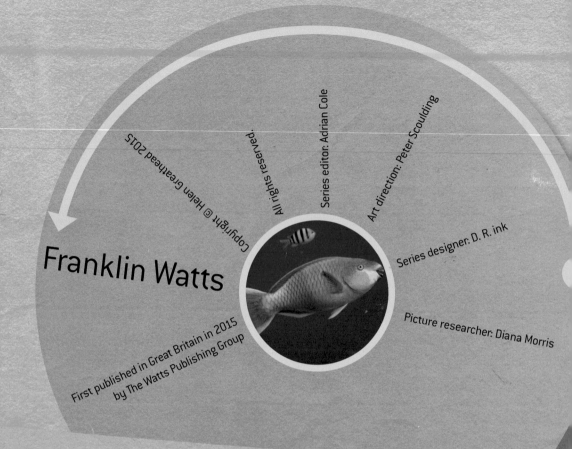

Franklin Watts

First published in Great Britain in 2015 by The Watts Publishing Group

Series editor: Adrian Cole

Art direction: Peter Scoulding

Series designer: D. R. ink

Picture researcher: Diana Morris

Photo credits

Jesse Albanese/Dreamstime: 9c. Andrew Allport/Dreamstime: 28t. arka38/Shutterstock: 24tr.astra88888/Dreamstime: 12b. Parawat Isurangura Na Ayudhaya/Dreamstime: 18r. Jeffrey Banke/Dreamstime: 29b. Rommel Canlas/Shutterstock: 14bl. Musat Christian/Dreamstime: 5bl. Cigdem Sean Cooper/Shutterstock: 25bl. Designpicssub/Dreamstime: 20t. Dennis W. Donahue/Shutterstock: 25cr. Dennis Donohue/Dreamstime: 23. Otto Duplessis/Dreamstime: 13br. Edurivero/Dreamstime: 28b. Michael Elliott/Dreamstime: 25tr. Michael & Patricia Fogden/Minden/FLPA: 25cl. Fotolotti/Dreamstime: 24tl. Fotomicar/Dreamstime: 25tl. Bonnie Frink/Dreamstime: 5br. Christos Georgiou/Shutterstock: 4b, 7b, 8ti, 27c. Dominique Gest/Biosphoto/FLPA: 30cr. Fred Goldstein/Dreamstime: 25br. Derek Gordon/Dreamstime: 17t. Frank Hildebrand/istockphoto: 8tr. Miroslav Hlavko/Shutterstock: 20b. Mitsuhiko Imamori/Minden Pictures/Corbis: 24bg, 24br. ink-k/Shutterstock: 24tc. Isselee/Dreamstime: 9b, 30tr. Jaymudallar/Dreamstime: 13cr. Cathy Keifer/Dreamstime: 15b. Kjetil Kolbjornsrud/Dreamstime: 27t. Vladimir Konjushenko/Dreamstime: 26. Brian Kushner/Dreamstime: 30cl. Jenny LeighW/istockphoto: 9t. Linagal/Dreamstime: 13t. Ilazarus/istockphoto: front cover r, 1r, 6b. R Gino Santa Maria/Dreamstime: 18l. Marog1981/Dreamstime: 30br. Matt9122/Shutterstock: 17b. Chris Moncrieff/Dreamstime: 21cl. Moolkum/Shutterstock: 30tl. Piotr Naskrecki/Minden Picture/FLPA: 30bl. Duncan Noakes/Dreamstime: 15t. Natalia Pavlova/Dreamstime: 13bl. photochecker/istockphoto: front cover l, 1l, 6t. Pitphotographs/Dreamstime: 21cr. Prillfoto/Dreamstime: 29t. Reuters/Corbis: 21tl. Filippo Romeo/Dreamstime: 14br. Tiu de Roy/Minden Pictures/FLPA: 16r. John Ruble/Wikipedia Commons: 5cr. Santisuh4/Dreamstime: 12t.Komprach Sapanrat/Dreamstime: 21tr. Shutterstock: 8b. Sandra van Der Steen/Dreamstime: 22. Marzanna Syncerz/Dreamstime: 27b. Marco Tomasini/Dreamstime: 13c. Sergey Uryandov/Dreamstime: 10b, 11b. Vladvitek/Dreamstime: 10t. Whitmore Farm: 5tr. Wikipedia Commons: 16c, 19.

Every attempt has been made to clear copyright. Should there be any inadvertent omission please apply to the publisher for rectification.

Dewey number 508
HB ISBN 978 1 4451 4204 3
Library ebook ISBN 978 1 4451 4206 7

Printed in China

Franklin Watts

An imprint of
Hachette Children's Group
Part of The Watts Publishing Group
Carmelite House
50 Victoria Embankment
London EC4Y 0DZ

An Hachette UK Company
www.hachette.co.uk
www.franklinwatts.co.uk

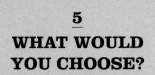

FAKE DEATH, LIKE A POSSUM
...OR FAINT LIKE
A GOAT?

WE CHOSE...

Faking death. A possum can keel over with its mouth open and produce green goo from its bottom, which even makes it smell like it's dead. Predators don't hang around! 'Fainting' goats, however, go stiff-legged when they are startled and fall over. It's something they can't control and isn't useful at all.

BALD HEAD
LIKE A CONDOR...
OR BALD RED BOTTOM
LIKE A BABOON?

WE CHOSE...

The red bottom. A condor's head is bald so its feathers don't get messy when it's feeding on rotting animal bodies. Nice! To male baboons, a female with a big red bottom looks like the perfect mate.

THE FACTS

ALLIGATORS:

- Measure up to 2.5 m
- Weigh an average of 450 kg
- Move fast – they can leap 1.5 m out of the water to grab lunch from the riverbank
- Have up to 80 teeth – they'll get through 2–3,000 in a lifetime!

SWIM WITH AN ALLIGATOR... OR A SHOAL OF PIRANHAS?

THE FACTS

PIRANHAS:

- Measure up to 30 cm
- Weigh up to 3.5 kg
- Can smell blood from 2 km away
- Are born with razor-sharp teeth – a shoal of piranhas can strip animal flesh down to the bone in minutes

SWIMMING WITH ALLIGATORS

An alligator will eat just about anything: fish, turtles, snakes, birds, frogs and small mammals are top of its menu. It might even swallow a small deer.

It probably wouldn't want to eat you. You'd be too big to swallow whole. Leave it alone, and it will usually just ignore you.

ALLIGATOR ATTACKS!

In 2006, in Florida, USA, three people were eaten by alligators. Twelve people were attacked altogether. That's way above average. There had been a drought. The hungry alligators were desperate for food.

If an alligator attacks – fight back! You might scare it away.

SWIMMING WITH PIRANHAS

Piranhas usually eat other fish – they might even attack small mammals or birds that wander into the water.

They probably won't bother you – unless they can smell your blood! Piranhas do strip human bodies of their flesh, but only when they're already dead.

PIRANHA ATTACK!

On Christmas Day 2013, a shoal of piranhas attacked a terrified crowd of swimmers in the sea in Brazil. Seventy people were hurt. One girl lost part of a finger. The attack was very unusual.

To prevent a piranha attack – don't go in the water where piranha swim in the dry season, or if you have a cut. Don't swim near fishing boats.

AND FINALLY...

In Florida, USA, 13 people were killed by alligators in 10 years. Even in Florida, the chances of an alligator attack are one in 24 million.

There has been only one reported death by piranha.

WE CHOSE

The piranhas. You could lose a toe, but you won't lose your life.

FLY LIKE A PEREGRINE FALCON...OR RUN LIKE A CHEETAH?

The peregrine falcon can dive for its dinner at breath-taking speeds of over 322 kph! It's not so fast chasing its prey on the straight, but still flies a steady 38–53 kph.

The cheetah on land can reach stunning speeds of up to 98 kph to catch its prey. Then it needs to rest before it eats. If larger cats come calling, the cheetah is too small and tired to defend itself.

AND FINALLY...

Cheetahs are dying out in the African savannahs, but around the world peregrines are thriving – even in the City of London!

WE CHOSE

The falcon. Why run when you can fly?

WHAT WOULD YOU CHOOSE?

CHAT TO A CHIMP... OR A PARROT?

WE CHOSE...

Chat to a parrot – it's easier! The parrot will learn to speak your language, though you might have to teach it first. The chimp can only communicate in sign language, so you'll need to learn to sign too.

Didn't you know?
A lost parakeet in Japan found its way home by telling the police where it lived!

BE A BEAUTIFUL DUNG BEETLE... OR A CATERPILLAR THAT LOOKS LIKE BIRD POO?

WE CHOSE...

The caterpillar. Dung beetles eat poo, live in it, roll in it, or tunnel through it all their lives. The caterpillar only looks like poo to put off predators, and it will, of course, turn into a beautiful butterfly.

CHANGE COLOUR LIKE A CHAMELEON... OR FAN OUT YOUR TAIL LIKE A PEACOCK?

WE CHOSE...

The peacock. A chameleon's skin colour isn't for camouflage. Colour shows up its mood – an angry chameleon might turn bright yellow to scare its enemy. The peacock fans out its colourful tail-feathers to attract a peahen.

Fight off mosquitoes by washing often, covering up with light-coloured clothes, eating garlic and wearing perfume.

THE FACTS

MOSQUITOES:
- Measure up to 2 cm long
- Weigh around 2.5 mg
- Live for up to six months
- Travel at roughly 2.4 kph
- Have no teeth; but can suck up blood that weighs three times as much as their own body

Didn't you know?
The annoying buzzing sound it makes is the mosquito beating its wings 300–600 times a second!

BE BITTEN BY A MOSQUITO...
OR A GREAT WHITE SHARK?

THE FACTS

GREAT WHITE SHARKS:
- Measure, on average, between 4.6–6 m long
- Weigh up to 2,268 kg
- Can live for 100 years!
- Zoom in for the kill at 56 kph!
- Have around 300 dagger-like teeth arranged in rows inside their jaws
- Found mostly in warm (12–24 degree) seas

Didn't you know?
Great white sharks can smell a single drop of blood in 100 litres of water.

WHAT WOULD YOU CHOOSE?

THE TRUTH ABOUT MOSQUITOES

Only egg-carrying female mosquitoes suck your blood – to feed protein to their eggs. They stab two tubes into your flesh. One tube delivers a liquid that stops your blood clotting; the other one sucks up the blood.

MOSQUITO BITES

There are 2,500 types of mosquito. Of these 430 are Anopheles, and 34 types of Anophele can infect humans with malaria. Mosquitoes sense your presence from the carbon dioxide you breathe out. They like sweaty people with stinky feet the best.

THE TRUTH ABOUT GREAT WHITES

They're actually grey on top; it's the belly that is white. Great whites are probably responsible for about 50 per cent of all shark attacks – they're one of the biggest fish in the sea.

GREAT WHITE BITES

The first bite the shark takes is usually a tester, to see if you're blubbery enough. If you're bony, it will probably swim away. Great whites think seals, sealions, dolphins and turtles are tastiest.

Avoid great white bites by swimming close to the shore in a group and don't swim if you're bleeding. In an attack, fight back. Bash and scratch where it hurts: the nose, the eyes and the gills.

AND FINALLY...

In 2012, malaria, transmitted by mosquitoes, killed around 627,000 people (mainly in Africa). In 2013 72 people were attacked by sharks – 10 of them died.

In parts of the ocean, great white sharks are endangered, but as the Earth warms, mosquito numbers are increasing.

WE CHOSE

The shark. You're more likely to die by getting malaria from a mosquito bite.

EAT SILKWORM PUPAE... OR SCORPIONS?

A silkworm in the 'pupa' stage is in its cocoon, waiting to turn into a moth. People in silk-producing countries, such as Thailand and Korea, eat the pupae, which are sold in supermarkets tinned, frozen or dried.

All scorpions have a sting in the tail. A few thousand people die every year from them, though not all scorpions are deadly. Weirdly, some people do eat raw scorpions, and Chinese street stalls display them live on sticks, ready to cook.

AND FINALLY...

Silkworm pupae don't smell too good, and eating them has been described as 'like chewing bones'. Pupae and scorpions are equally healthy to eat, and better for the planet than meat. The scorpions are deep-fried. They taste a bit like crab or shrimp – and the sting is chopped off before cooking!

WE CHOSE

Scorpions. Especially if they come with chilli sauce!

Didn't you know?
1,900 species of bug have now been identified as safe to eat.

WHAT WOULD YOU CHOOSE?

PLAY WITH A CASSOWARY... OR BE WARY OF IT?

WE CHOSE...

Be wary! Cassowaries can grow to nearly 2 m tall. They can't fly, but can jump up high and run at up to 50 kph. If one thinks you're a threat it could charge and slash you with its razor-sharp claw. However, the last death by cassowary was in 1926.

STEP IN FOX ...OR WOMBAT POO?

WE CHOSE...

Wombat poo. It comes out square (so it doesn't roll away) and it's very dry and clean. It's so full of plant fibres that it can be recycled to make paper. Steer clear of fox poo. It smells disgusting, and carries diseases which can be passed on to humans – ew!

LAUGH LIKE A HYENA...OR A RAT?

WE CHOSE...

The rat. Tests have shown that rats make high-pitched, happy chirping sounds when a human hand tickles their tummy. When a spotted hyena makes sounds we think are laughter, it's actually fighting for food.

A TRUNK LIKE AN ELEPHANT...
OR A TONGUE LIKE A CHAMELEON?

THE FACTS

A CHAMELEON'S TONGUE:
- Is one and a half times as long as its body
- Can shoot out of the mouth at 21.5 kph
- Moves so fast, it can capture insects, moths and even small lizards, birds and snakes using the sticky tip of its tongue and the power of suction
- Never misses – as long as conditions are right

THE FACTS

AN ELEPHANT'S TRUNK:
- Is fantastically flexible with over 40,000 muscles!
- Can grow up to 2 m long and suck up 9 litres of water
- Has two nostrils and either one or two fingers at its tip
- Is like your upper lip and nose extended into one long bendy tube

WHAT CAN A TRUNK DO?

The elephant can lift a heavy load, eat, smell, drink, feel, breathe and make sounds through its trunk. It can use it to hug a friend or fight an enemy, to shower itself with water, or spray itself with dust.

HOW DOES THE TONGUE WORK?

Muscles in the chameleon's tongue work together with collagen tissue, which stretches like elastic. The collagen is wrapped in layers around the tongue bone, and attaches to the accelerator muscle that propels the tongue out of the mouth. The sticky tip then latches on to its prey.

Having a super-speedy tongue means the slow-moving chameleon can creep up on its prey and catch it from a safe distance.

AND FINALLY...

An elephant's trunk is amazing, but sometimes a trunk gets in the way – baby elephants trip over them! The chameleon's tongue disappears neatly inside the mouth, only coming out when it's needed.

An elephant's trunk can lift five per cent of its bodyweight; a chameleon's tongue can lift ten per cent of its bodyweight!

WE CHOSE

The chameleon's tongue. Imagine being able to snatch a chip from your teacher's plate across the dinner hall without anybody knowing you did it!

Didn't you know?
When elephants go underwater they use their trunk like a snorkel.

CLIMB A GIANT SEQUOIA...
OR A SANDBOX TREE?

The giant sequoia has been called the largest living organism on Earth. The tree can grow to over 90 m tall, and nearly 9 m wide. The sequoia loves cool mountain-top conditions, but survives summer bushfires because its bark doesn't catch fire! Beware of hornets nesting in the branches though.

The sandbox tree can grow up to 30 m tall, and produce half-metre wide leaves. Its fruit looks like a mini pumpkin and explodes with a loud crack when it is ripe, scattering the seeds up to 30 m away.

AND FINALLY...

It won't be easy to climb a sequoia. You'll need ropes, a helmet and a human guide, but the views will be worth it. The sandbox tree is nicknamed the 'dynamite tree' because its fruit explode. Its bark is covered in vicious spikes and is poisonous — along with its sap, seeds and leaves!

WE CHOSE

Climb a giant sequoia. Just make sure those saftey ropes are tied on!

A PELICAN AS YOUR BIG BROTHER... OR A SAND TIGER SHARK?

Baby pelicans compete for food from their mum's and dad's beaks. The parents can never bring enough to feed them all, so the biggest bird, male or female, turns on the smaller siblings, pecking them, fighting them and even pushing them out of the nest – to certain death.

When a sand tiger shark hatches in its mother's womb it begins to gobble up its smaller siblings, along with any eggs that haven't hatched! Only one baby shark survives. The shark is so well fed when it is born that it's already a whopping 1 m long.

AND FINALLY...

If you're not the biggest pelican your chances of survival are slim. Sand tiger sharks usually give birth to two sharks at a time, from two separate wombs!

WE CHOSE

The sand tiger shark. If your brother is a sand tiger shark, you'll be just as big and nasty as he is!

BUMP INTO A BOX JELLYFISH ...OR A GIANT HORNET?

THE FACTS

BOX JELLYFISH:
- Are cube-shaped, measuring up to 20 cm on each side
- Have 24 eyes
- Trail 60 tentacles that grow up to 3 m long
- Weigh up to 2 kg

Didn't you know?
Hornet venom can be used to ease arthritis!

THE FACTS

ASIAN GIANT HORNETS:
- Can grow up to 5 cm long
- Have four eyes
- Have a 6 mm long stinger
- Are about 20 times heavier than bees

Didn't you know?
One box jellyfish contains enough venom to kill 60 people!

WHY DO JELLIES STING?

Box jellies trail their tentacles to ensnare their food. The deadly sting paralyses its victims to prevent a death struggle damaging the delicate tentacles.

HOW MUCH DOES IT HURT?

In humans the intense burning pain can send the body into shock, triggering a heart attack and death within three minutes.

WHAT CAN YOU DO?

Wear tights in certain waters, or a stinger suit. If stung, vinegar can stop the poison seeping into your body, but you need to apply it fast.

Jellyfish attacks: Box jellies don't set out to harm humans, but they do kill up to 40 people a year in the Philippines alone.

HOW DO HORNETS ATTACK?

Groups of giant hornets attack honeybees. They tear the bees apart to get protein for their larvae. Thirty hornets can kill 30,000 bees in just three hours!

HOW MUCH DOES IT HURT?

Human victims say the sting feels like a red-hot nail in your body – it leaves a hole where it has eaten away body tissue. Multiple stings can cause kidney failure.

WHAT CAN YOU DO?

Wear dull colours and no perfume. If you disturb a hornet, don't run. Crouch down, cover your head and stay very still.

Hornet attacks: Hornets don't usually target humans, but in 2013 across three cities in China hornets attacked over 1,600 people: 42 died.

AND FINALLY...

If you bump into a hornet and stay calm there's a chance it won't sting. Bump into the wrong type of box jellyfish and each tentacle has 5,000 cells that will sting.

WE CHOSE

The hornet. It might sting you, but it won't (usually) kill you.

Didn't you know?
Horned lizards dig into the soil to sleep. They use their nose like a spade and can bury themselves up to 10 cm deep.

SQUIRT BLOOD LIKE A LIZARD...
OR SHED YOUR TAIL-SKIN
LIKE A DORMOUSE?

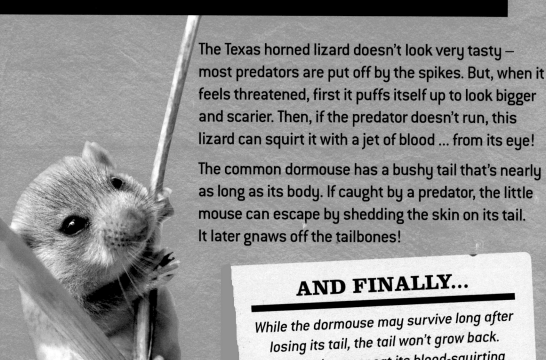

The Texas horned lizard doesn't look very tasty — most predators are put off by the spikes. But, when it feels threatened, first it puffs itself up to look bigger and scarier. Then, if the predator doesn't run, this lizard can squirt it with a jet of blood ... from its eye!

The common dormouse has a bushy tail that's nearly as long as its body. If caught by a predator, the little mouse can escape by shedding the skin on its tail. It later gnaws off the tailbones!

AND FINALLY...

While the dormouse may survive long after losing its tail, the tail won't grow back. The lizard can repeat its blood-squirting defence again and again.

WE CHOSE

The lizard. The dormouse gets one shot only.

WATCH A FOOTBALL MATCH PLAYED BY ELEPHANTS... OR PENGUINS?

WE CHOSE...

The elephant football match (at a festival in Nepal). It's much more exciting. The elephants run, shoot and score goals (though they do have riders on their backs). The penguins play a slower game, on a smaller pitch and are easily distracted!

BE AS CLEAN AS A PIG... OR A SLOTH?

WE CHOSE...

A pig – they don't sweat, so they cool off in mud or water. The mud also keeps little critters away. Moths and algae living in a sloth's fur make it turn slime green! Both animals separate their food stores from their toilets, though.

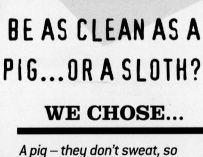

COME FACE TO FACE WITH A HIPPO...OR A GRIZZLY BEAR?

THE FACTS

A COMMON HIPPO:
- Can weigh over 3,250 kg and grow to more than 4 m long
- Eats up to 85 kg of grass each day
- Lives in water and on land – it can run more than 32 kph
- Has up to 40 teeth – the largest ones are for fighting!
- Can kill a crocodile with one sharp bite

WHEN HIPPOS ATTACK

A hippo is more likely to attack at the end of the dry season, when food and water are harder to find. If a hippo yawns, roars, rears or shakes its head, it's getting angry.

HIDE, CLIMB, RUN

Avoid a hippo attack by keeping your distance. A hippo doesn't like to be surprised. If one spots you, climb up a tree, or hide behind a handy termite mound. Alternatively, try to out-run it. Hippos can't run fast for long. Head for a nearby building or vehicle, or change direction suddenly and run for the bushes. Hippos are supposed to be vegetarian, but they do sometimes eat meat.

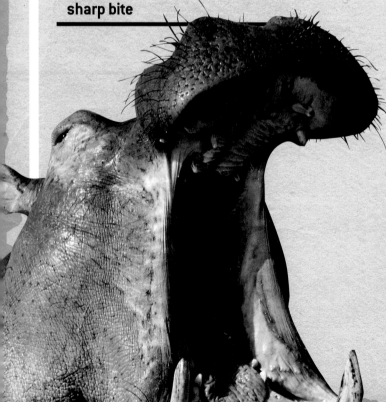

WHAT WOULD YOU CHOOSE?

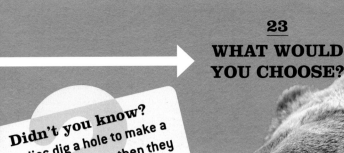

Didn't you know?
Grizzlies dig a hole to make a den for hibernation, then they sleep for seven months without eating or going to the toilet!

WHEN GRIZZLIES ATTACK

A grizzly may attack if it is surprised, thinks you are threatening its cubs or want its food. Beware when a bear pushes back its ears and looks you right in the eye.

WHAT TO DO

Avoid bear attacks by singing or talking loudly as you walk – the bear will know you are coming and move away. If it keeps coming, back away slowly, talking calmly all the time. If it starts to charge, drop facedown on the ground, pull in your knees and cover your head with your arms. Only fight back if the bear doesn't leave you alone.

THE FACTS

A GRIZZLY:
- Can weigh over 360 kg and measure up to 2.5 m long
- Likes to eat seeds, berries, animals, fish, insects, grasses and roots
- Can run at 48 kph!
- Can smell a dead animal miles away
- Has claws up to 13 cm long

AND FINALLY...

In the USA, bears of all kinds are responsible for 1–2 deaths a year, on average. Figures for hippo attacks vary, but they may cause up to 400 human deaths a year.

WE CHOSE

The grizzly. It won't be a fair fight – so play dead!

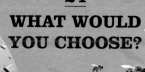

Didn't you know?
In Israel, one way of dealing with the locusts is to fry them up and eat them with barbecue sauce!

BE CAUGHT IN A SWARM OF LOCUSTS ...OR HONEYBEES?

Locusts are a type of grasshopper that often live happily on their own. However, when conditions are right, locusts can gather in vast groups, change their form and take off on the rampage together. A swarm of locusts can cover over 730 square km of land, with up to 80 million locusts in just 80 square metres!

Honey bees swarm to find a new home if their hive gets overcrowded. A breakaway group of up to 50,000 creates a second queen, and then flies away.

AND FINALLY...

Bees don't usually sting unless they feel threatened. Locusts don't bite (or sting), but they'd starve you to death. Each locust eats its own weight in crops every day. Once the swarm moves on the crops are gone!

WE CHOSE

The honeybees. In a swarm, don't swat them, cover your neck and face and try to run away.

WHAT WOULD YOU CHOOSE?

GROOM A GIBBON... OR A GRIN AT A CAPUCHIN MONKEY?

WE CHOSE...

Groom a gibbon – this is friendly behaviour that helps keep gibbons healthy, getting rid of irritating insects, dead skin and dirt. The capuchin monkey (and other monkeys) would see your grin as aggressive behaviour: baring your teeth means you want to fight!

A FROG AS A DAD...OR A LION?

WE CHOSE...

The frog. If food is scarce a lion dad will let his family starve. After a mum frog lays her eggs, however, the dad Darwin's frog swallows them, keeping them in his throat for protection. He spits them back out when they are fully formed frogs.

SLEEP IN THE SEA LIKE AN OTTER... OR A PARROTFISH?

WE CHOSE...

The sea otter. It floats on its back in the water, wrapping itself up in a blanket of seaweed and even holding hands with a mate so it doesn't drift away. The parrotfish sleeps in a protective bubble ... made from its own mucus – or snot!

SING LIKE A NIGHTINGALE...
OR HOWL LIKE A WOLF?

THE FACTS

NIGHTINGALES:

- Measure up to 17 cm long with a wingspan of up to 24 cm
- Nest among stinging nettles, blackberries and sand dunes
- Look a bit dull, but...
- Sing beautifully – and very loudly
- Know over 200 different tunes

Didn't you know?
In 1924 the BBC recorded an unusual duet. Beatrice Harrison played her cello and a nightingale sang – a million people listened on their radios.

WHAT ARE THEY SINGING ABOUT?

It's only the male bird that sings. During the daytime he chirrups to protect his territory, but at night, when most other birds go quiet, he carries on singing, often for hours on end. At night he's hoping to attract a mate. Female birds are like *X-Factor* judges: they're looking for the best performance.

WHAT WOULD YOU CHOOSE?

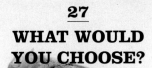

THE FACTS

WOLVES:
- Belong to the dog family
- Measure up to 180 cm from the nose to the tip of the tail
- Have hardly ever attacked humans – even though we've feared them for centuries
- Hunt in packs of six to ten

WHAT ARE THEY HOWLING FOR?

Being nocturnal, wolves also sing (or howl) at night. Lifting up their heads helps carry the howl up to 16 km, if no trees get in the way. A wolf howls to call the pack together, to let the pack know where it is and to attract a mate.

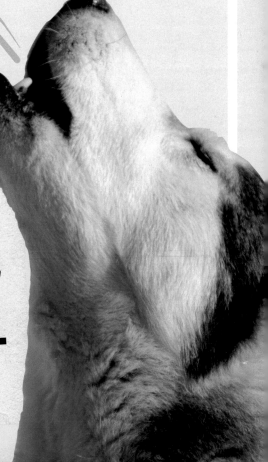

AND FINALLY...

Night-time singing sessions can take it out of a bird and might even make it lose weight. Also, the singing doesn't just attract a mate, it gets a predator's attention too! A wolf howl can confuse predators. A group of howling wolves creates an eerie harmony that makes a small pack sound much bigger than it really is.

WE CHOSE

Howl like a wolf. You won't be a hit with the neighbours, but you'll be a howling success with your pack.

A HORN LIKE A RHINO... OR A BEAK LIKE A TOUCAN?

Didn't you know? 22nd September is World Rhino Day.

The longest rhino horns can grow to a phenomenal 1.5 m. A female uses her horns to protect her babies. A male uses his in combat. He can take on a buffalo or a lion, and fight another rhino to the death.

The toucan's beak grows up to 19 cm long. It's hollow, so not great for fighting. Instead, the beak controls the temperature in the toucan's body, drawing heat from the body into the beak so that the body stays cool.

AND FINALLY...

Poachers hunt rhinos and hack off their horns to sell. The toucan's rainforest habitat is disappearing, and many are captured as pets.

WE CHOSE

The beak. You could lose your freedom, but you won't lose your beak.

Didn't you know?
The biggest recorded bald eagle nest weighed nearly 3 tonnes!

NEST LIKE AN EAGLE
...OR BURROW LIKE A MEERKAT?

A bald eagle's ideal nest is in the forked branch of the tallest tree, with great views over the forest. A nearby lake is a handy place to catch fish for its ever-hungry eaglets. The nest is built with sticks and lined with grasses, moss and feathers.

Meerkat burrows are networks of tunnels in the ground where a group of 20 or more meerkats can escape the hot, dangerous desert. The tunnels lead to cool bedrooms up to 2 m below ground. The burrows have many entrances. Meerkat guards signal with a bark when it's safe to come out.

AND FINALLY...

Meerkats keep moving home because their burrows become infested with ticks and fleas! Bald eagles often return to their comfy nest each year, repairing and improving it.

WE CHOSE

The nest. One nest was used for 34 years!

POISONED SPINES LIKE A PORCUPINE... OR TOUGH SCALES LIKE A PANGOLIN?

WE CHOSE...

Pangolin scales. Porcupines can fall out of trees and stab themselves with their own quills. Scaly pangolins can curl up into an armour-plated ball – which no predator can penetrate – and simply roll away from danger!

FALL IN LOVE WITH A TURTLE DOVE... OR A VULTURE?

WE CHOSE...

A Vulture. Mating pairs stick together for ever, while recent research has shown that even though they're symbols of love, turtle doves do not! Black vultures may not look so cute, but they even take turns to look after the chicks.

REGENERATE LIKE A STARFISH...OR A WORM?

WE CHOSE...

The worm. When a starfish loses a limb another grows in its place. If a planarian worm loses its head it will grow another one, complete with brain and even old memories!

Didn't you know?
Scientists call starfish 'sea stars', because they aren't really fish, they are echinoderms.

WHAT WOULD YOU CHOOSE?

GLOSSARY

anaphylactic shock – A serious, life-threatening allergic reaction, including a severe rash, vomiting and/or swelling of the throat.

bushfire – A fire in a forest or wooded area that spreads fast in hot weather.

collagen – Body tissue which is strong and flexible.

drought – Long period of time without any rainfall.

echinoderm – The name for the group of animals that live in the sea and don't have a backbone, including starfish, sea urchins and sea cucumbers.

habitat – The natural place where an animal or plant lives.

larva (larvae plural) – The stage of an insect's lifecycle between egg and pupa (see below).

malaria – A disease carried by mosquitoes which causes fever.

nocturnal – Animals that sleep during the day and are active at night.

peahen – The name for a female peacock.

predator – An animal that hunts other animals in order to eat them as food.

pupa (pupae plural) – The stage of an insect's lifecycle between larva (e.g. a caterpillar) and adult (e.g. a butterfly).

sap – The liquid inside plants that transports food to all the cells of the plant.

savannah – A flat grassy area, usually in Africa.

shoal – The name for a group of fish.

sibling – Another word for brother or sister.

womb – The part of a female animal's body where her baby or babies form and grow.

WEBSITES

http://animals.nationalgeographic.com/animals/
Photographs, videos and information about animals of the world.

http://ngkids.co.uk/
The National Geographic children's website.

http://www.bbc.co.uk/nature/animals
Videos and photos from the BBC.

http://news.bbc.co.uk/1/hi/world/south_asia/8435112.stm
Watch some elephant football (page 21).

http://www.bbc.co.uk/programmes/p010svl2
Hear a nightingale singing a duet with a cello (page 26).

http://www.worldrhinoday.org/
Find out more about endangered rhinos and World Rhino Day.

INDEX

GARDEN PLANNING
AND
PLANTING

by
Eigil Kiaer
with
Hans Petersen

English edition supervised and edited by
Anthony Huxley

Illustrations by
Verner Hancke

BLANDFORD PRESS
POOLE   DORSET

First published in the English edition 1976

World copyright © 1975
Politekens Forlag A/S, Copenhagen

English text © 1976 Blandford Press Ltd.
Link House, West Street
Poole, Dorset BH15 1LL

ISBN 0 7137 0792 5

Printed in Great Britain by Richard Clay
(Chaucer Press) Ltd, Bungay, Suffolk

Colour plates printed in Denmark

CONTENTS

PREFACE

This book is intended to be a natural companion to four previous books in the same series – *Garden Annuals and Bulbs*, *Garden Perennials and Water Plants*, *Deciduous Garden Trees and Shrubs* and *Evergreen Garden Trees and Shrubs*. In each of these titles the aim was to show plants in possible settings and to clarify their eventual size and shape. In this book, the plants specified in the plans are largely those represented in the four companion books.

Garden planning is not as simple as it may appear. The first essential is to know how plants will develop. All too often, plants are placed far too close together without much thought to the colours that will result, and without enough consideration of their effect in the whole garden scene.

This book was prepared by the landscape gardener Eigel Kiaer who, with the horticultural advisor Hans Petersen, wrote the original Danish text. The colour plates were prepared by Verner Hancke. The text was translated from the Danish by Mrs. Gillian Hartz and has been adapted and edited for English language readership by horticultural expert Anthony Huxley.

In this edition plant variety names used in Britain have been adopted and common English names are used where possible. A list of the Latin names of plants and flowers is given with their common English equivalents on page 222.

As in the companion volumes, the names are given in accordance with the International Code of Nomenclature for Cultivated Plants. In this, the technical Latin name is printed in italics. Following this there may be the name of a garden variety. In the case of naturally occurring wild varieties, this third name will also be in italics. Where the plant is of garden origin, however, the name is printed in ordinary type between inverted commas, e.g. *Arabis caucasica* 'Rosabella'. This treatment occurs even where the name of the cultivar (as garden varieties are officially called) is in Latin, as in *Juniperus communis* 'Hibernica'.

7

However, it should be emphasised that throughout the book, the varieties are only suggestions. There are, among annuals and roses for example, many varieties of similar appearance and colouring which could be used in the garden plans. This would be a matter of availability and personal preference.

INTRODUCTION

Whenever a garden is to be newly laid out and planted, the first basic problem is that of the choice of style; secondly there is the detailed layout scheme; and thirdly the selection of trees, shrubs, flowers and other plants. Unless the owner has already laid out several gardens it is more than likely that his knowledge of the many possibilities is certain to be inadequate.

Any garden – whether large or small – should be an expression of the owner's taste and love of gardening (or otherwise!) and should also take economy into consideration. For example, it would be ridiculous to plan a complicated garden full of flowers which demand constant attention throughout the year, if the family only intends to use it for relaxation during the summer months. A 'leisure garden' can be just as beneficial to some people as a garden with fruit, vegetables and flowers is to the family which prefers a 'functional garden' where full use is made of every available piece of soil.

The Choice of Garden Style

As will be seen from the colour plates in this book, there are a great many possibilities to choose from when it comes to types of garden. Therefore, think very carefully before making a final decision on any particular scheme.

The aim of illustrating all these ideas in colour is first and foremost to give the gardener the possibility of choosing exactly the right type of garden plan for his family. This is of the utmost importance since the garden will be there for many years.

Some of the colour plates show planting details which will be of especial interest to the owner whose garden is already well established but who wishes to give it added variety and interest.

Regardless of the type of garden scheme chosen, it is always wise to work out a detailed plan before starting work. In this way the work can be undertaken at one's leisure over two or three years.

Drawing a plan
It is practical to draw the details of the plan on a piece of squared graph paper, e.g. where each 1 × 1 cm square corresponds to 1 sq. m in the garden (i.e. a scale of 1:100). Having drawn in the house and the boundary lines and marked the points of the compass, use circles to indicate trees and shrubs in the manner shown in the colour plates. The size of the circles should denote the space required by the trees and shrubs in, say, 10–15 years time. In this way one is certain to leave sufficient room for the plants to develop naturally. You will soon discover that there is really space for far fewer plants and trees than you originally thought possible.

When the layout for the scheme has been decided upon, it would be wise to begin by planting the trees, larger shrubs, and hedges if the garden is not fenced. The plants forming the undergrowth should be planted next, between the shrubs. Finally, roses, herbaceous and rock plants should be placed as required. These can also be drawn on a plan, using a larger scale (1:50 or even 1:20). All this work can easily stretch over two or three years, during which time the soil can be prepared and kept free from weeds. A lawn can be sown or turfed immediately after the trees and larger shrubs have been planted; or alternatively it can wait until last and thus be made more or less free from weeds.

The Selection of Plants

The range of trees, shrubs, perennials, annuals, bulbs and tubers is so wide and varied that it is often difficult to choose the relatively small number for which there will be room in the average garden. But apart from this, once one has selected the plants one likes, the problem arises as to how they should be arranged to best advantage and be able to develop freely without crowding out each other. In order to solve this problem, it is necessary to acquire a basic knowledge of plants, their natural habitat and growth form.

Thus, seek as much information as possible about the plants

one has chosen. This is particularly important with regard to trees and shrubs as they will remain in the same place for many years, and it is obviously essential to visualise how tall and wide these will become in 10–15 years time.

One of the aims of this book is to give the owner this information in an easily understood form and this is the purpose of the first few colour plates: Plates 1–3 illustrate the shapes of common trees, shrubs and perennials; Plates 4–9 are used purely to illustrate the effective use of colour when arranging plants in the garden.

The arrangements in Plates 10–13 should be considered 'exercises' until one actually starts arranging one's own garden plants. They can either be copied exactly or used to inspire one's own arrangements.

As most houses have a front garden it would be wise to study Plates 14 and 15, and realise that the front garden should not use all the inspiration or money. Plates 16–30 will be of interest for the owner who has already established his garden, but who wishes to make a few changes here and there. These plates illustrate the growth of plants along walls or hedges, the effective grouping of trees and shrubs, and the planting of flowerbeds with roses, perennials, annuals, bulbs and tubers.

The rest of the colour plates should be considered as suggestions: some for whole gardens, some for 'original' layouts which can be a separate entity within a garden. There is something for all tastes – a garden with flowers for cutting, a green garden, a meadow of flowers, a lily garden, a kaleidoscopic garden, a place for rock plants, a herb garden, a Japanese garden, a scheme for ornamental grasses, a garden for butterflies, a cubist garden – to name but a few. It cannot be overemphasised that a garden should be limited to one, or at the most two, of the illustrated schemes. Some suggestions are also given for the garden of a holiday house, and finally for balcony and roof gardens and window-boxes.

The captions and notes contained in the colour plates should be read in conjunction with the descriptive text for each illustration. These text sections (starting on p. 145) are sub-titled and numbered in exactly the same way as the colour plates.

Readers will notice throughout a strong emphasis on the desirability of ground-cover planting rather than bare earth wherever possible. Bare earth means weed invasion and accompanying work. Once established, ground-cover plants largely eliminate weeds, as long as any persistent, deep-rooting kinds have been eradicated before planting begins.

The most important ground-cover plant, perhaps, is *Vinca minor*, lesser periwinkle. This is very hardy and shade-loving, but at the same time tolerates a rich flora of underplanted bulbs and tubers – even winter aconites can surmount its green leaves. There is an attractive variegated form. Its relation *V.major* makes much longer shoots so is not suited to bulb planting, though it has luxuriant growth. Other useful low ground-cover plants are *Cotoneaster dammeri*, *Pachysandra terminalis* and *Hedera helix*, ivy, in considerable variety.

If one can bear to leave out bulbs, then *Cotoneaster hybridus* 'Skogholm' is well suited for underplanting larger shrubs. It spreads quickly and layers itself. *Hypericum calycinum*, Rose of Sharon, is another very vigorous plant, with attractive golden flowers if grown in sun. All too rarely seen, *Waldsteinia ternata* is a low, pale green cover plant with many runners which produce a mass of yellow flowers in spring. It is, by the way, very easy to propagate as one just pushes shoots into the ground. Equally to be recommended are *Asarum europaeum*, asarabacca (aptly known in Denmark as Viking's helmets) and *Asperula odorata*, sweet woodruff.

If there is plenty of space it is worth trying *Lamium galeobdolon variegatum*, yellow archangel, which is evergreen in spite of its herbaceous appearance. It has beautiful silver-marked leaves and stout yellow deadnettle flowers in spring. It is most successful under very vigorous shrubs. *L.maculatum*, the variegated deadnettle with white-marked leaves and pink flowers, is rather less vigorous but an excellent weed suppressor.

Ground cover can be relieved with small groups of shade-loving perennials such as *Astrantia major*, masterwort, *Hosta fortunei* and others, plantain lilies, *Polygonatum multiflorum*, Solomon's seal, *Rodgersia pinnata* and *R.tabularis*. Shade-loving plants are seldom as colourful as sun-lovers but their leaves are often large and decorative. It is the abundant foliage which gives an impression of lushness which a garden in the sun may lack. And shade-lovers can have lovely flowers, as for instance *Cimicifuga racemosa*, black snake-root, and *Ligularia przewalskii*, which are both very elegant.

*   *   *   *   *

This book is based on the many years of experience and acquired knowledge of the authors and editor. Personal experience, so vital if one is to have a really attractive garden, is most easily gained by visiting other people's gardens. In the U.K. many are open to the public for various charities or under the auspices of The National Trust. There are also public parks, botanical gardens, arboreta, and in particular the garden of The Royal Horticultural Society at Wisley, Surrey, and that of the Northern Horticultural Society at Harlow Car, near Harrogate. There are many horticultural shows where plants can be seen and ordered, and of course nurseries and garden centres where they can be seen growing.

COLOUR PLATES

Juniperus
Chamaecyparis

1 The Shapes of Trees

Trees have many different habits of growth. There are pyramidal and pillar-shaped trees such as fir, cypress, poplar and thuja (**1-4**), large broad-crowned trees like oak, elm, lime and pine (**5-8**), and trees with drooping branches such as the weeping willow (**9**). Special cultivation techniques can produce distinctive forms like the gnarled pot-grown bonsai (**10**), and clipped box and yew (topiary) (**11**).

Shrubs also have many habits of growth. Some like *Rosa rugosa* (**1**) have a broad, close-twigged form while others like *Juniperus communis* 'Repanda' (**3**), *Cotoneaster dammeri* and *C. horizontalis* (**4-5**) and *Hypericum calycinum* (**9**) have low, spreading or creeping habits. *Rosa hugonis* (**6**) has tall, broad, slightly drooping growth in contrast to *Syringa vulgaris* (**7**) which is tall and compact. Other contrasting habits are twisted hazel, *Corylus avellana* 'Contorta' (**8**) and dwarf Spruce, *Picea glauca* 'Conica' (**10**), and the little Japanese Quince, *Chaenomeles japonica* (**2**) of low, spreading growth.

1   2   3   4

Growth habits of perennials are just as varied as those of trees and shrubs. For example, the giant miscanthus, mullein, foxtail lily (eremurus), yucca and red hot poker (**1-5**), are erect and bold and should be isolated to give greatest effect. Others, such as asters, erigeron, phlox, helenium and rudbeckia (**6-10**), form broad, close clusters and have many flowers, often massed in clusters. They can be used to advantage in flowerbeds where an attractive colour scheme is important.

Of all the colours in the garden, green is the most important. However, not all shades complement each other. The blue-green and grey-green shades of the silver fir (**1**), Atlas cedar (**2**), grey poplar (**3**), white poplar (**4**), blue fescue grass (**5**) and oleaster (**6**) do not blend well with the lusher greens of iris (**7**), yew (**8**), bamboo (**9**), ivy (**10**), box (**11**) and vines (**12**).

5 Flowers with Warm Colours

Yellow, orange and red are 'warm' colours. They are found in calendula
(**1**), evening primrose (**2**), geum (**3**), helenium (**4**), tagetes (**5**), mullein
(**6**), *Primula florindae* (**7**), pansy (**8**), geranium (**9**), nasturtium (**10**) and
oriental poppy (**11**). The reddish-purple shades found in michaelmas
daisies (**12**), phlox (**13**) and peony (**14**) form a transition between the
'warm' and the 'cold' colours.

The 'cold' colours – blue, violet, pink and white – occur in cornflowers (**1**), delphiniums (**2**), echinops (**3**), regal lily (**4**), lily of the valley (**5**), clematis (**6**), iris (**7**) and gentian (**11**). They do not always complement the 'warm' colours. Exceptions are the bluer shades of purple and mauve flowers such as michaelmas daisies (**8-9**) and campanulas (**10**), which can be used with both 'warm' and 'cold' colours.

In natural surroundings, flowers often vary in colour according to their position, be it woodland, wayside or stony areas. Gardeners can learn from this and place the pale, more delicate flowers – for example lilies (**2**), aquilegia (**3**), lily of the valley (**4**), bleeding heart (**5**) and honeysuckle (**6**) – in shady positions. Ivy (**1**) is very much a shade-loving plant.

In warm, sunny places one would expect to find brightly coloured flowers. These are the most effective conditions for wisteria (**1**), rudbeckia (**2**), dahlias (**3-4**), ageratum (**5**), salvia (**6**), tagetes (**7**) and lobelia (**8**).

For a plant to stand out well against its background it is necessary to think carefully about the colour of the plants behind and around it. An unfortunate grouping of several colours can have just the opposite effect. The two examples on the left show how a background of shades of green, a peaceful atmosphere is created (*top*) or how a very dark background of yew and cushions of aubrieta in the foreground creates a harmonious colour effect (*below*). The colour of the tulips stands out more strongly here. Along the walls of the house one has to be particularly careful, especially with red brick walls, which could be a disastrous background for pink and red roses.

An arrangement confined to just the 'warm' shades of yellow, orange and red can be extremely effective. In the examples on the right, the following flowers have been used: *Solidago* 'Golden Wings' (**1**), *Rudbeckia nitida* (**2**), *Dahlia* 'Yellow Hammer' (**3**), *Lantana camara* (**4**), *Gazania splendens* (**5**), *Tagetes patula* 'Rusty Red', 'Sunny' and 'Harmony' (**6-8**), *Dahlia* 'David Howard' (**9**) and *Achillea filipendulina* 'Coronation Gold' (**10**). Pretty effects can also be created using shades of other colours – blues, violets and pinks of *Aster amellus*, delphiniums, perennial erigerons, *Salvia superba* and *Sedum spectabile*. A particularly outstanding effect is achieved using the pink, purple and mauve forms of phlox and *Aster novi-belgii* Michaelmas daisies with *Gypsophila repens*, *Ageratum houstonianum* and *Verbena venosa*.

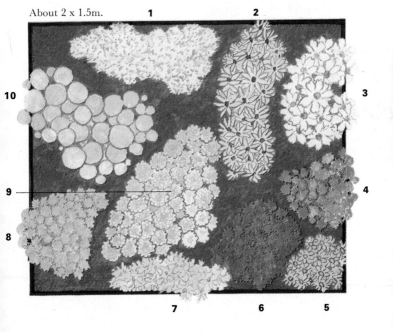

About 2 x 1.5m.

When planting herbaceous borders, pick a bunch of the flowers concerned and as shown above, it will be seen how well the colours blend. Here *Aster amellus* 'Moerheim Gem' (**1**), *Echinops ritro* (**2**), *Heliopsis scabra* 'Patula' (**3**), and *Oenothera missouriensis* (**4**) are planted in small beds with 3-5 sorts in each bed at the most.

About 1.5 x 1.5m

While the herbaceous border on the left shows some of the prettiest late summer perennials, the group below shows the bright colours of mid-summer: *Papaver orientale* 'Storm Torch' (**1**), *Delphinium* 'F. W. Smith' (**2**), *Chrysanthemum maximum* 'Universal' (**3**) and *Erigeron* 'Wuppertal' (**4**). Similarly, one can design a spring and early summer bed by 'picking a bunch of flowers'.

bout 1.5 x 1.5m

If several types of plants are to form a group, then a well-balanced effect can be achieved in many ways, examples of which are given here and in Plates 11-13. One can, as is shown here, choose plants with similar leaves and so produce a subtle and peaceful atmosphere. The plants have leaves of more or less the same basic sort: *Catalpa bignonioides* (**1**), *Ligustrum vulgare* 'Atrovirens' (**2**), *Syringa vulgaris* 'Souvenir de Louis Spaëth' (**3**) and *Lonicera pileata* (**4**).

1   **2** **4**   **3**

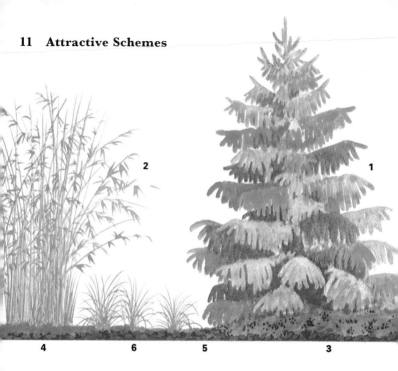

It is wise to let one or two larger shrubs or trees be the dominating plants and let the rest complete the picture. As shown above, the handsome weeping spruce *Picea brewerana* (**1**) stands out with a graceful group of bamboos (**2**) keeping it company. *Cotoneaster horizontalis* (**3**), *Lonicera pileata* (**4**) and *Vinca major* (**5**) form the decorative ground-cover with a few specimans of the ornamental grass *Miscanthus sinensis* 'Gracillimus' (**6**), giving added interest.

About 5 x 2m.

he arrangement above is effective during summer, autumn and winter. The little
mach, *Rhus typhina* 'Laciniata' (**1**), is the dominant plant with the evergreen
pericum calycinum (**2**) beneath it. On the right there are roses – *Rosa carolina* and
sa moyesii (**3-4**) – which bear both beautiful flowers and pretty hips. If preferred
ese could be replaced by the evergreen *Cotoneaster salicifolius floccosus* which bears red
rries. The ground cover is *C. dammeri*.

This emphasises the strong contrast between a pale, flowering tree (**1**), such as Japanese cherry or a crab apple, and a dark green background of, for example, box holly or yew (**2**). The sombre dark green would also emphasise a *Daphne mezereu* (**3**) and a *Magnolia stellata* (**4**) with some pretty spring bulbs (**5-6**), e.g. the tul 'China Pink' and the narcissus 'Ice Follies'. The ground cover is *Scilla hispanica* (**7**).

bout 5 x 2m.

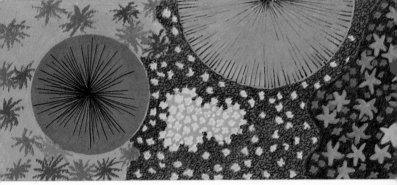

ere it is the evergreen *Cryptomeria japonica* 'Lobbii' (**1**) and *Chamaecyparis pisifera*
ilifera' (**2**) which give character to the beautiful surroundings. Several types of
ather (**3**) have been planted around the first tree, handsome day lilies (**4**), and low
rubby cinquefoil (*Potentilla fruticosa*) (**5**) around the other tree. *Hypericum calycinum*
) and *Vinca major* (**7**) are used as ground cover, but one could just as effectively have
ed a cotoneaster through which eranthis and scillas could have peeped in the spring.

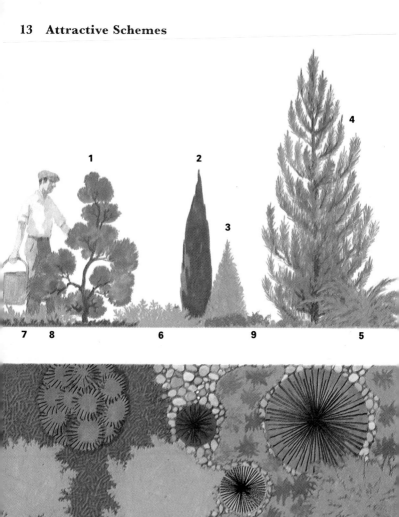

A selection of conifers of distinctive shape has been planted relatively far apart
allow space for free development without hampering each other: *Chamaecyparis obtu*
'Erecta' (**1**), *Juniperus communis* 'Hibernica' (**2**), *Picea glauca* 'Conica' (**3**) and *Pir*
cembra (**4**). *Juniperus media* 'Pfitzerana aurea' (**5**), *Picea abies* 'Nidiformis' (**6**) a
Juniperus communis 'Repanda' (**7**) form the ground cover together with *Lonicera pilea*
(**8**) and *Erica carnea* varieties (**9**)

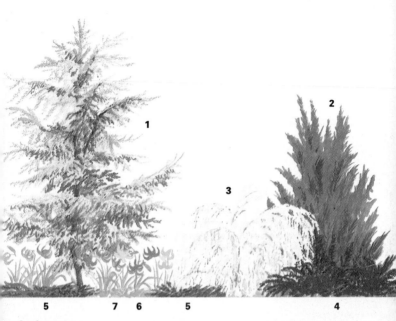

out 5 x 2m.

...re we see how the blue-grey Atlas cedar, *Cedrus atlantica* 'Glauca' (**1**) will dominate ...arrangement and the other plants' colours and shapes should be chosen to com-...ment it. The companion plants are *Juniperus squamata* 'Meyeri' (**2**), *Cytisus praecox* ...*C. purpureus* (**4**), *Juniperus horizontalis* 'Glauca' (**5**) and various lilies (**6**) such as ...*um martagon*, *L. regale* and *L. speciosum*. The ground cover is the silver-grey, white ...vering *Cerastium biebersteinii* (**7**).

On modern housing estates it is usual to leave a front garden which faces the road open and without a fence – or just separated from the road by a low supporting wall or a white 'ranch' fence. One ought to keep the plan as simple as possible, using only a few types of plant. The ground between these can be turfed or planted with ground cover. In the above examples *Picea omorika* (**1**), *Laburnum watereri* (**2**), *Juniperus communis* 'Repanda' (**3**), *Rhododendron catawbiense* (**4**), *Cotoneaster salicifolius floccosus* (**5**) and *Lonicera henryi* (**6**) have been used, the last two plants trained up the walls of the house.

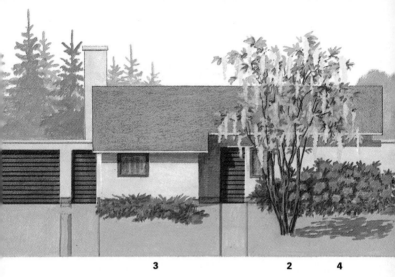

3   2   4

About 20 x 8m.

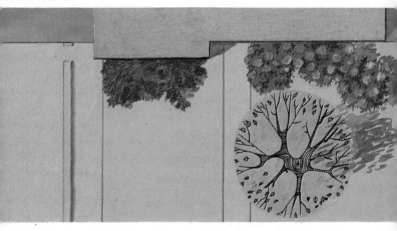

The appearance of an estate, as a whole, will be most attractive and park-like if the gardens on both sides of the road use shrubs and trees of similar appearance. This sort of scheme can be planned well in advance and so one can have an estate of attractive roads of widely differing appearance. For example, one road could use flowering magnolias (say *Magnolia kobus*) predominantly, while another could produce the splendid colour contrasts of a Japanese flowering cherry with dark bushes of yew. The same 'rules' apply to plants used along low supporting walls, but clearly such schemes must depend on cooperation between neighbours.

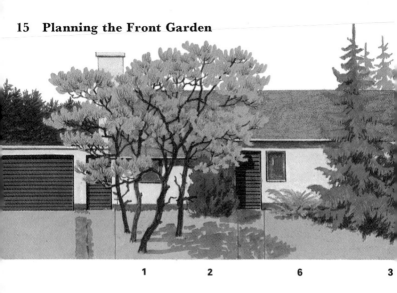

1   2   6   3

If there is room, quite strong-growing trees can be used effectively in groups, though large quick-growing trees such as horse chestnut, weeping willow and Lombardy poplar should be avoided. *Pinus sylvestris* (**1**), *Juniperus virginiana* 'Glauca' (**2**), *Picea omorika* (**3**), *Chamaecyparis lawsoniana* 'Allumii' (**4**) and *Rhus typhina* 'Laciniata' (**5**) have been used in the examples. Walnut trees and many flowering cherries are also suitable. In the background, see how the closely planted lilac, fir, yew, or similar trees of medium height, produce a complete and peaceful arrangement.

About 20 x 8m.

When choosing shrubs for the open-plan front garden, select those which will tolerate the constant traffic of children and dogs. In the above illustration, different varieties of *Juniperus media* 'Pfitzerana' (**6**) and *J. communis* 'Repanda' (**7**) have been used. Sometimes it may be advisable to use some thorny shrubs in the front garden and some of the berberis family would be ideal, e.g. *Berberis aggregata*, *B. julianiae*, *B. stenophylla*, *B. thunbergii* and *B. verruculosa*. The last named is suitable should one wish to have a low hedge facing the road.

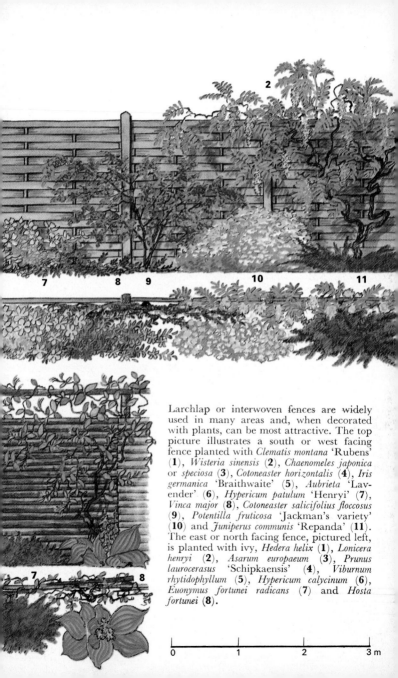

Larchlap or interwoven fences are widely used in many areas and, when decorated with plants, can be most attractive. The top picture illustrates a south or west facing fence planted with *Clematis montana* 'Rubens' (**1**), *Wisteria sinensis* (**2**), *Chaenomeles japonica* or *speciosa* (**3**), *Cotoneaster horizontalis* (**4**), *Iris germanica* 'Braithwaite' (**5**), *Aubrieta* 'Lavender' (**6**), *Hypericum patulum* 'Henryi' (**7**), *Vinca major* (**8**), *Cotoneaster salicifolius floccosus* (**9**), *Potentilla fruticosa* 'Jackman's variety' (**10**) and *Juniperus communis* 'Repanda' (**11**). The east or north facing fence, pictured left, is planted with ivy, *Hedera helix* (**1**), *Lonicera henryi* (**2**), *Asarum europaeum* (**3**), *Prunus laurocerasus* 'Schipkaensis' (**4**), *Viburnum rhytidophyllum* (**5**), *Hypericum calycinum* (**6**), *Euonymus fortunei radicans* (**7**) and *Hosta fortunei* (**8**).

0   3   6   9   12m

If your house is situated far back on a plot, so that a broad drive to the house is necessary, a border of shrubs and perennials can form an attractive and welcoming screen. The accompanying illustration shows the use of *Viburnum fragrans* and *V. carlesii* (**1-2**), *Corylopsis willmottiae* (**3**), *Hamamelis japonica* (**4**), *Ribes sanguineum* and *R. alpinum* (**5-6**), *Rhododendron praecox* (**7**), *Daphne mezereum* (**8**), *Prunus subhirtella* 'Autumnalis' (**9**), *Cornus mas* (**10**), *Forsythia intermedia* 'Lynwood' (**11**) and *Taxus baccata* (**12**). The *Cotoneaster dammeri* (**13**), *Erica carnea* (**14**), *Adonis vernalis* (**15**), *Viola odorata* (**16**) and *Vinca minor* (**17**) are used as ground cover with Siberian squill, crocuses, narcissi and tulips giving added interest. *Jasminum nudiflorum* (**18**) and *Cotoneaster salicifolius floccosus* (**19**) have been trained up the fence with the neighbouring garden. Grass has been allowed to grow between the flagstones.

1   2   3   4   5

1   2   3   4

1   2   3   4

18   Planting Along Low Walls

6   7   8

Walls of this sort, which should not be higher than 50-100cm (20-40 in.), can be built of various materials. Here, the top wall is of uniform concrete blocks or reconstituted stone. Red and yellow bricks would also be attractive. The middle illustration shows a wall made of slabs of rock. The bottom wall is of boulders and is really only suitable in rural areas. When choosing plants for low walls, buy several plants of the same species for each wall. This is far more effective than planting a motley selection. Remember also that the plants chosen should require little nourishment and be able to tolerate dryness and widely varying temperatures.

5   6

The top wall is planted with *Aubrieta* 'Dr. Mules' (**1**), *Cytisus praecox* 'Allgold' (**2**), *Potentilla fruticosa* 'Tangerine'' (**3**) *Campanula poscharskyana* 'Stella' (**4**), *Gypsophila repens* 'Rosea' (**5**), *Alyssum saxatile* 'Flore pleno' (**6**), *Aubrieta* 'Lavendar' (**7**), and *Centranthus ruber* 'Atrococcineus' (**8**).

The middle wall is planted with *Dianthus plumarius* 'Duchess of Fife' (**1**), *Campanula portenschlagiana* (**2**), *Juniperus communis* 'Repanda' (**3**), *Aubrieta* 'Dr. Mules' (**4**), *Phlox subulata* 'G. F. Wilson' (**5**) and *Cotoneaster adpressus praecox* (**6**).

6   7   8

The bottom wall is planted with *Cerastium biebersteinii* (**1**), *Linum perenne* (**2**), *Arabis caucasica* 'Rosabella' (**3**), *Juniperus horizontalis* (**4**), *Campanula portenschlagiana* (**5**), *Geum* 'Mrs. Bradshaw' (**6**), *Potentilla arbuscula* (**7**) and *Linaria pallida* (**8**).

0	0,5	1 m

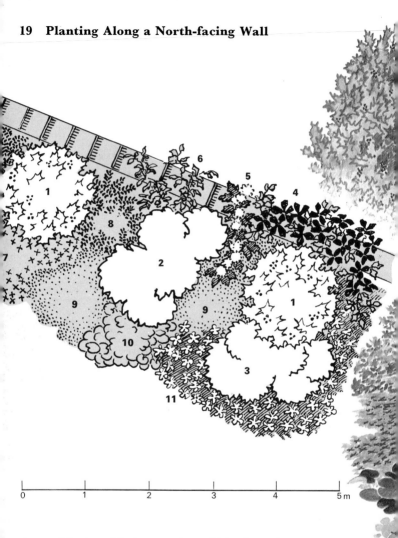

A row of shrubs and herbaceous plants which tolerate shade is most suitable for planting along north – facing walls or fences. As a rule, annuals and roses will not thrive where the earth usually remains cold until well into the summer (the yellow rose 'Mermaid' is an exception which enjoys a northern aspect). Along the wall on the right, *Ilex aquifolium* (**1**), *Viburnum rhytidophyllum* (**2**), *Prunus laurocerasus* 'Otto Luyken' (**3**), *Clematis* 'Jackmannii' (**4**), *Hydrangea petiolaris* (**5**) and *Lonicera periclymenum* 'Serotina' (**6**) have been chosen. The ground cover consists of *Vinca major* (**7**), *Lonicera pileata* (**8**), *Asperula odorata* (**9**), *Asarum europaeum* (**10**) and *Hypericum calycinum* (**11**).

Conditions along a south-facing wall are usually regarded as the best with rega[r]
to soil temperature. If the moisture level is adequate very few plants will not gro[w]
well under these conditions. Along this wall have been planted *Gypsophila panicula[ta]*
'Bristol Fairy' (**1**), *Lavandula officinalis* (**2**), *Clematis* 'Nelly Moser' (**3**), *Hibisc[us]*
syriacus 'Woodbridge' (**4**), *Sedum rupestre* (**5**), *Iris germanica* 'Braithwaite' (**6**), *Sal[ix]*

superba 'East Friesland' (**7**), *Achillea filipendulina* 'Coronation Gold' (**8**), rose 'Golden Showers' (**9**), *Aubrieta* 'Lavender' (**10**), *Arabis caucasica* 'Rosabella' (**11**), *Yucca filamentosa* (**12**), *Sempervivum tectorum* (**13**), *Sedum spectabile* 'Autumn Joy' (**14**), *Aubrieta* 'Dr. Mules' (**15**), *Alyssum saxatile* 'Flore pleno' (**16**), *Buddleia davidii* 'Magnifica' (**17**), *Centranthus ruber* 'Atrococcineus' (**18**) and *Aubrieta deltoidea* (**19**).

21 Conifers

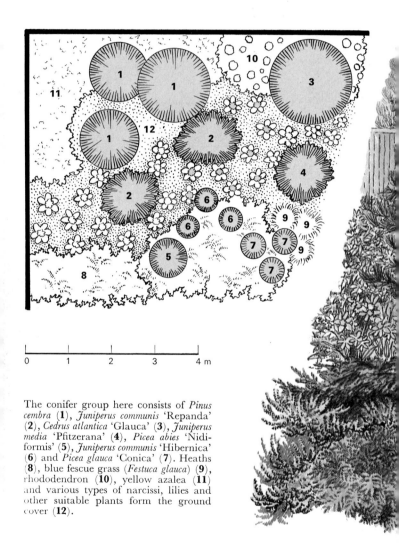

The conifer group here consists of *Pinus
cembra* (**1**), *Juniperus communis* 'Repanda'
(**2**), *Cedrus atlantica* 'Glauca' (**3**), *Juniperus
media* 'Pfitzerana' (**4**), *Picea abies* 'Nidiformis' (**5**), *Juniperus communis* 'Hibernica'
(**6**) and *Picea glauca* 'Conica' (**7**). Heaths
(**8**), blue fescue grass (*Festuca glauca*) (**9**),
rhododendron (**10**), yellow azalea (**11**)
and various types of narcissi, lilies and
other suitable plants form the ground
cover (**12**).

Most coniferous trees and shrubs look at their best when planted in groups. They
are economical with regard to soil and nourishment and thrive best in a light,
sandy soil with not too high a lime content. In contrast to other evergreen trees

and shrubs, which as a rule tolerate some shadow, conifers prefer a light, airy position in the garden. The above arrangement would be suitable in a garden near the coast (not too exposed) or a residential area with ground sloping gently to the sunniest direction.

To hide a wall, fence, etc., in the garden, use a group of evergreen trees and shrubs. Firs and pines become thin and straggly and do not like the shade and will not thrive with leaf-bearing species. The group here consists of *Ilex aquifolium* (**1**), *Prunus laurocerasus* 'Otto Luyken' (**2**), *Rhododendron* 'Rosamundi' (**3**), *Mahonia*

aquifolium (**4**) and *Cotoneaster salicifolius floccosus* (**5**). The ground cover is *Lonicera pileata* (**6**), asarabacca (*Asarum europaeum* (**7**), *Hypericum calycinum* (**8**) and *Gaultheria procumbens* (**9**). Box would also have been suitable if it is kept low trimmed.

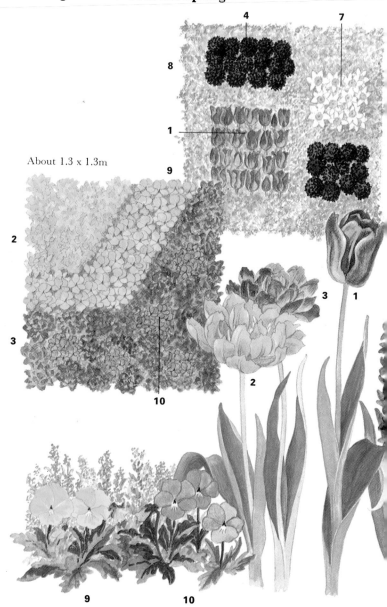

About 1.3 x 1.3m

The shape of colourful spring beds can be square, rectangular or circular, but regardless of shape should not be less than 1 sq m (about 10½ sq. ft.) in area, and preferably two or three times larger. The following flowers are recommended: Tulips 'Queen of Bartigons' (**1**), 'Theeroos' (**2**) and 'Peach Blossom' (**3**); the deep blue hyacinth 'Ostara' (**4**); and narcissi 'Rembrandt' (**5**), 'Ice Follies' (**6**) and 'Queen of Bicolors' (**7**). The groundwork is of forget-me-not (**8**) and yellow and lavender pansies (**9-10**). The choice of tulips is a simple matter, as long as the colours blend well together. Bright orange and red tulips, for example, would spoil the effect of beds like these.

About 1.5 x 1.5m

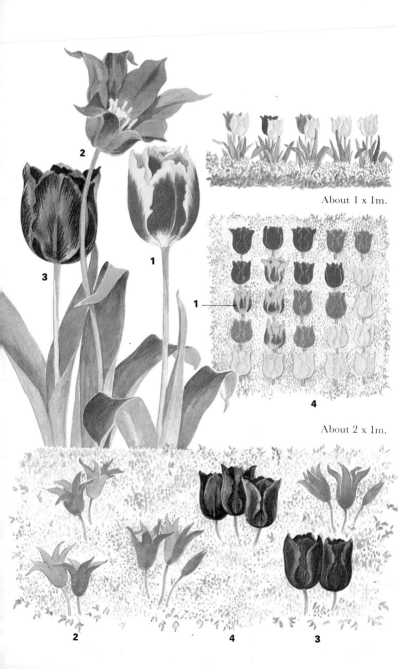

About 1 x 1m.

About 2 x 1m.

24 Bright Flowerbeds for Spring

Low, early flowering tulips are pretty when planted in rows, but tall, late flowering varieties look best in small groups. The top bed on the left contains 'Keizerskroon' (**1**) and other red, orange and yellow types such as 'Cassini' and 'Bellona'. The bottom bed on the left is planted with 'China Pink' and 'Demeter' (**2-3**). In both cases, the groundwork is of forget-me-not (**4**). In the lower bed are *Fritillaria imperialis* (**5**), coloured primroses (**6**), aubrieta (**7**), *Scilla hispanica* (**8**) and *Primula denticulata* and *P. veris* (**9-10**).

About 1.5 x 1m.

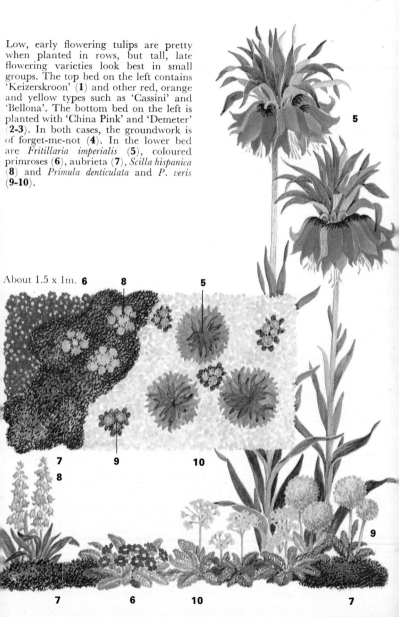

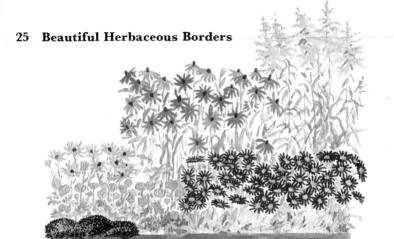

Herbaceous borders should not be less than 2 sq. m (2½ sq. yds) in area as illustrated here in these unusual formalised square beds in a sunny lawn. The plants are *Geum* 'Mrs. Bradshaw' (**1**), *Aster frikartii* 'Wonder of Stafa' (**2**), *Rudbeckia speciosa* (**3**), *Aubrieta* 'Dr. Mules' (**4**), *Trollius* 'Goldquelle' (**5**), *Helenium* 'Moerheim Beauty' (**6**), *Aster amellus* 'Moerheim Gem' (**7**), *Solidago* 'Leraft' (**8**), *Heuchera sanguinea* 'Pluie de Feu' (**9**) and *Viola cornuta* (**10**). These give a display over a long period.

About 2 x 1.5m

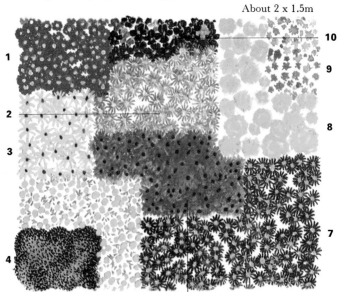

Tall, decorative perennials, or bulbous and tuberous plants, should be surrounded by low, herbaceous subjects. The group here consists of *Phlox subulata* 'G. F. Wilson' (**1**), *Lilium martagon* (**2**), *Anemone hybrida* 'Queen Charlotte' (**3**), *Sedum spectabile* 'Brilliant' (**4**), *Viola cornuta* (**5**), *Gypsophila repens* 'Rosea' (**6**), *Thalictrum dipterocarpum* (**7**), *Dianthus plumarius* 'Duchess of Fife' (**8**), *Erigeron* 'Wuppertal' (**9**), *Scabiosa caucasica* 'Miss Willmott' (**10**) and *Aubrieta deltoidea* (**11**).

About 2 x 1.5m

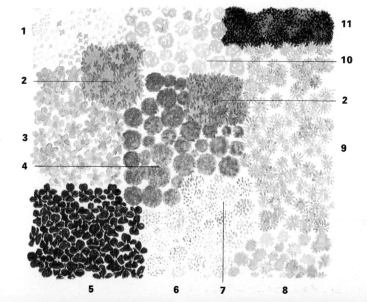

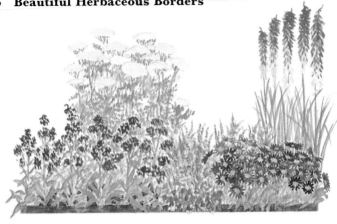

When planning herbaceous borders, remember that they ought to flower throughout the summer. This is an arrangement of *Aster amellus* 'King George' (**1**), *Achillea filipendulina* 'Coronation Gold' (**2**), *Oenothera tetragona* (**3**), *Centranthus ruber* 'Atrococcineus' (**4**), *Campanula portenschlagiana* (**5**), *Aster alpinus* 'Beechwood' (**6**), *Salvia superba* 'East Friesland' (**7**), *Geum* 'Goldball' (**8**), *Alyssum saxatile* 'Flore pleno' (**9**) and *Kniphofia* 'Fireflame' (**10**).

About 2 x 1.5m.

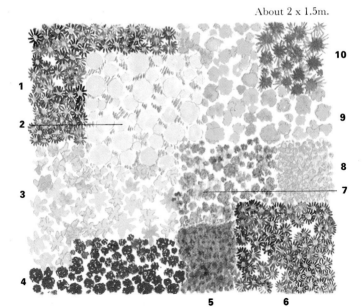

The bed here will be in flower from spring until autumn. Perennials used are *Veronica incana* (**1**), *Phlox* 'Jules Sandeau', 'Widar', 'Olive Wells Durrant', 'Starfire', 'Excelsior', 'Sternhimmel' and 'Mia Ruys' (**2-7**), *Viscaria vulgaris* 'Splendens Plena' (**8**), *Iris pumila* 'Cyanea' (**9**), *Campanula carpatica* (**10**), *Linum perenne* (**11**) and *Dianthus plumarius* 'Gloriosa' (**12**), with a group of tall tulips and yellow pansies (**13-14**) in the middle. These last can be replaced by a few annuals in June.

About 2 x 1.5m.

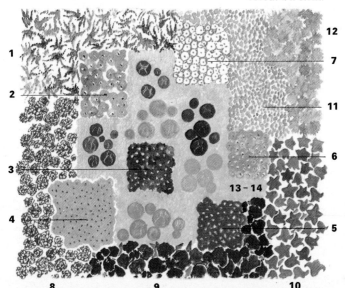

Spring's gay beds can be replaced by beds just as colourful in summer. The
flowers here have strong, bright colours all in the 'warm' tones. A bed of this
sort should be placed in the foreground of the garden. *Lobelia* 'Cambridge
Blue' (**1**), *Tagetes patula* 'Sunny' and 'Flash' (**2-3**), *Ageratum houstonianum*
'Imperial Dwarf' (**4**), *Dahlia* 'Symphonia' (**5**) nad gladioli 'Life Flame', 'Peter
Pears' and 'Flowersong' (**6-8**) have been used in this arrangement.

About 2 x 1.5m.

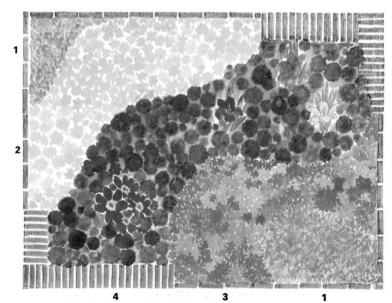

The bed which is shown here illustrates the effective use of pastel shades. This bed looks best set back in the garden. The plants are *Alyssum maritimum* 'Violet Queen' (**1**), *Tagetes patula* 'Petite Yellow' (**2**), *Begonia semperflorens* 'Indian Maid' (**3**), *Verbena venosa* (**4**), *Felicia amelloides* (**5**), 'White Favourite' (**6**) and gladioli 'Fancy Free', 'Blue Conqueror' and 'Peter Pears' (**7-9**).

About 2 x 1.5m

These roses all have 'warm' tones and are 'Europeana' (**1**), 'Peer Gynt' (**2**), 'Allgold' (**3**), 'Super Star' (**4**) and 'Summer Holiday' (**5**). Between the roses are tagetes (**6**), purple salvia (**7**), aubrieta (**8**), ageratum (**9**), campanula (**10**), cerastium (**11**), gypsophila (**12**) and lobelia (**13**).

Pink and white roses are most beautiful when planted in beds on their own. Here we have 'Pascali' (**1**), 'Iceberg' (**2**), 'Cricri' (**3**) and 'Pink Peace' (**4**), underplanted with ageratum (**5**), campanuala (**6**), cerastium (**7**), small-leafed thyme (**8**), periwinkle (**9**) and aubrieta (**10**) in between.

About 8 x 3m.

The bed on the left contains 'Fragrant Cloud' (**1**), 'Chinatown' (**2**), 'Evelyn Fison' (**3**), 'Hanne' (**4**), 'Korona' (**5**), 'Whisky Mac' (**6**) and 'Sutter's Gold' (**7**), most of which are scented. Some evergreen bushes – cherry laurel (**8**), holly (**9**) and mahonia (**10**) – have been planted to set off the roses. The ground cover consists of periwinkle and creeping gaultheria (**11-12**), with scillas and other bulbs planted in between.

The selection of flowers for cutting is
very wide. In a large garden it would
be wise to confine these plants to a
particular part of the garden so that
they can be sown and planted in rows
with narrow stone paths in between.
This makes for quick, easy picking,
even in wet weather An example of
this type of garden is shown on the
right. The following bulb and
tuberous plants have been used:
dahlias 'Good Morning', 'La Cierva',
'Oslo', 'Sonja', 'Goldelse', 'Gerry
Hoek', 'Requiem', 'Purple King',
'Yellow Hammer', 'Komet', 'White
Favourite', 'Bestseller', 'Brandaris'
and 'Top Mix' (**1-14**); annuals and
perennials are *Rudbeckia bicolor*
'Superba' (**15**), *Callistephus chinensis*
(China aster) (**16**), *Verbena venosa*
(**17**), *Scabiosa atropurpurea* (**18**), *Calendula officinalis* 'Orange King' (**19**),
Chrysanthemum coccineum 'E. M. Robinson' (**20**), *Lagurus ovatus* (**21**), *Nigella
damascena* (**22**), *Cosmos bipinnatus* (**23**)
and *Erigeron* 'Darkest of All' (**24**).
Note that the same grouping has
been used in several places within
the arrangement. The colour range
could have been widened by planting
late flowering tulips between the
dahlias, and room could have been
left for some roses suitable for cutting.
In addition, a long row of galdioli is
also recommended.

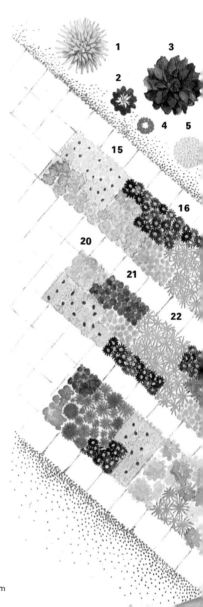

0   1   2   3 m

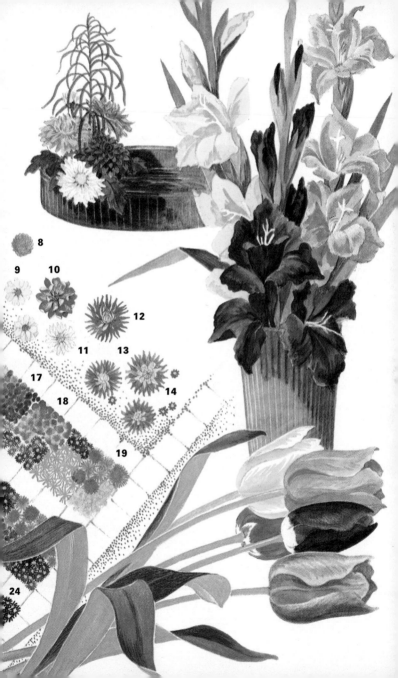

0   1   2   3   4   5 m

In a large garden it may be interesting to enclose an area, say 75 sq. m (90 sq. yds), with a beech hedge, and plant it with large trees, the crowns of which can be cut so that a roof of leaves is formed. If desired a pergola-like structure could be created in the crowns. Always select trees with beautiful leaves, for example red oak (**1**), tulip tree (**2**), walnut (**3**) and Norway maple (**4**).

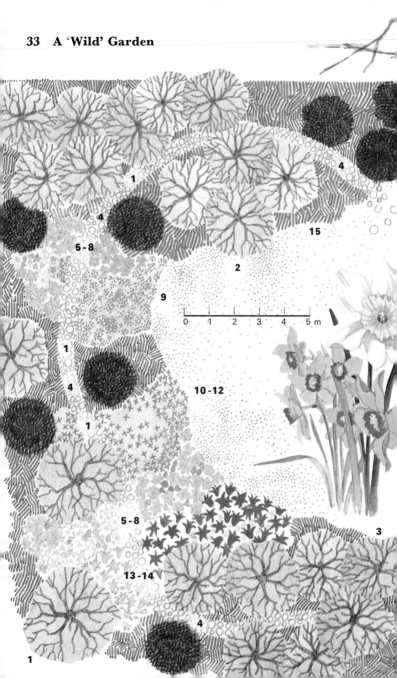

1

4

5 - 8

9

2

15

1

4

1

10 - 12

0   1   2   3   4   5 m

5 - 8

3

13 - 14

4

1

The garden containing apparently natural groupings of perennials, bulbs and tubers between light trees and shrubs has gradually become popular with many gardeners. Apart from silver birch, bird cherry, locust (*Gleditsia*) and yew (**1-4**), groups consisting of narcissi 'Scarlet Elegance' and 'Ice Follies', foxgloves, turk's-cap lilies (**5-8**), *Anchusa myosotidiflora* (**9**), woodruff, bugbane (*Cimicifuga*) and ostrich-plume fern (**10-12**), and tulips 'China Pink' and 'West Point' (**13-14**), have been planted. *Primula florindae* and *Thalictrum dipterocarpum* would also be suitable. The ground cover is *Lonicera pileata* (**15**).

Apart from lilies, the plants in a lily garden should include graceful perennials, ferns and grasses. Unusual hardy orchids and bulbs would also be suitable. Some possible lilies are *Lilium martagon* (**1**), *L. umbellatum* (**2**), *L. candidum* (**3**), *L. tigrinum* (**4**), *L. regale* (**5**), *L. speciosum* (**6**) and *L.* 'Destiny' (**7**). Among these *Miscanthus sinensis* 'Giganteus' and 'Gracillimus' (**8-9**), *Sinarundinaria murielae* (**10**), *Phyllitis scolopendrium* (**11**), *Polygonatum multiflorum* (**12**) and *Thalictrum dipterocarpum* (**13**) have been planted. Between the lilies, *Cotoneaster dammeri*, *Vinca minor*, lilies of the valley, early bulbs and ferns form the ground cover.

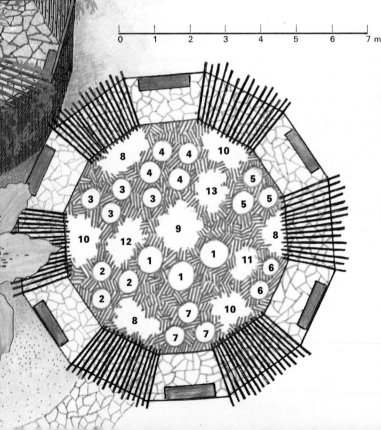

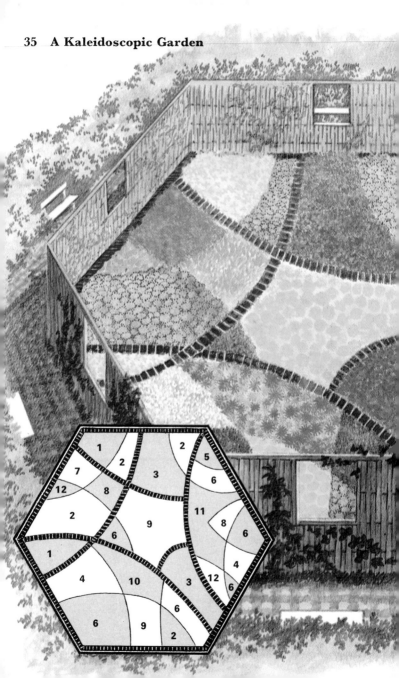

The kaleidoscope garden should consist solely of low, profusely flowering annuals, using only one type in each section, framed with dark stones or bricks. *Sanvitalia procumbens* (**1**), *Ageratum houstonianum* 'Imperial Dwarf' (**2**), *Begonia semperflorens* 'Sheila' and 'Snowbank' (**3-4**), *Salvia splendens* 'Violet Crown' (**5**), *Verbena venosa* (**6**), *Alyssum maritimum* 'Violet Queen' (**7**), *Senecio cineraria* (**8**), *Tagetes patula* 'Sunny' and 'Flash' (**9-10**), *Lantana camara* (**11**) and *Lobelia erinus* 'Crystal Palace' (**12**) have been used here. The idea was inspired by the kaleidoscope, an optical toy. While with the toy one turns the bottom of the kaleidoscope to change the gaily coloured pattern, with the garden one must walk from one peephole to another to achieve a similar result. Sun and shade will enhance the mosaic effect which the flowers produce.

0	1	2	3	4	5	6m

36 A Sunken Rockery

The old-fashioned rockery does not always suit the owner of a modern garden. On the other hand, you can grow a number of rock plants using this idea in a sunny corner of the garden. This provides excellent conditions for these plants and, at the same time, you have a warm place to sit undisturbed by neighbours. Remember that the sunken area should be well-drained and the earth be mixed with very coarse gravel before planting. The walls and 'tower' can be built of broken concrete slabs. A couple of juniper bushes (**1-2**) form the background for the stone bench. Within a group of Serbian firs *Picea*

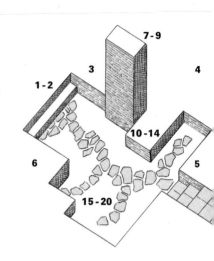

omorika (**3**), Arolla pines *Pinus cembra* (**4**), a Japanese maple (**5**) and shrubby cinquefoil (**6**), rock plants are grown. These include *Alyssum saxatile* 'Flore pleno', *Campanula portenschlagiana* and *Phlox subulata* 'Lilacina' (**7-9**), *Arabis caucasica* 'Rosabella', *Aubrieta* 'Dr. Mules', *Potentilla aurea*, *Saxifraga* 'Peter Pan' and *Sedum spathulifolium* (**10-14**), and *Cytisus praecox* 'Hollandia', *Hosta fortunei*, *Primula denticulata* and *Sempervivum heuffelii* (**15-18**). The tall *Verbascum densiflorum* and *Yucca filamentosa* (**19-20**) complete the picture.

Herbs are popular not only as flavouring but because they are also rich in vitamins. In the small herb garden illustrated above, the following are grown: sage (**1**), thyme (**2**), caraway (**3**), aniseed (**4**), sorrel (**5**), fennel (**6**), dill (**7**), mint (**8**), chamomile (**9**), lovage (**10**), chives (**11**), marjoram (**12**), lavender (**13**), lemon balm (**14**), tarragon (**15**), water cress (**16**), basil (**17**), parsley (**18**), savory (**19**) and rosemary (**20**). All these herbs grow best in a sunny position in light soil. Some, such as parsley and basil, must be grown annually from seed.

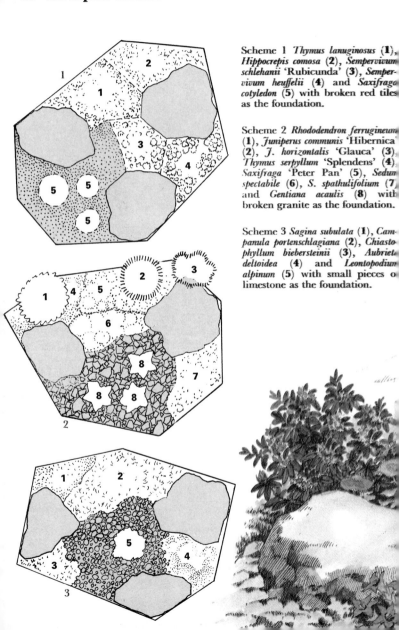

Scheme 1 *Thymus lanuginosus* (**1**), *Hippocrepis comosa* (**2**), *Sempervivum schlehanii* 'Rubicunda' (**3**), *Sempervivum heuffelii* (**4**) and *Saxifraga cotyledon* (**5**) with broken red tiles as the foundation.

Scheme 2 *Rhododendron ferrugineum* (**1**), *Juniperus communis* 'Hibernica' (**2**), *J. horizontalis* 'Glauca' (**3**), *Thymus serpyllum* 'Splendens' (**4**), *Saxifraga* 'Peter Pan' (**5**), *Sedum spectabile* (**6**), *S. spathulifolium* (**7**) and *Gentiana acaulis* (**8**) with broken granite as the foundation.

Scheme 3 *Sagina subulata* (**1**), *Campanula portenschlagiana* (**2**), *Chiastophyllum biebersteinii* (**3**), *Aubrieta deltoidea* (**4**) and *Leontopodium alpinum* (**5**) with small pieces of limestone as the foundation.

Instead of planning large rockeries in the garden, a much prettier effect is created by an arrangement of small separate alpine gardens. Each of the small gardens shown on the left is only about 1.5–2 sq.m (16–21 sq. ft).

Scheme 2

Section

Plan

0   1   2 m

Section

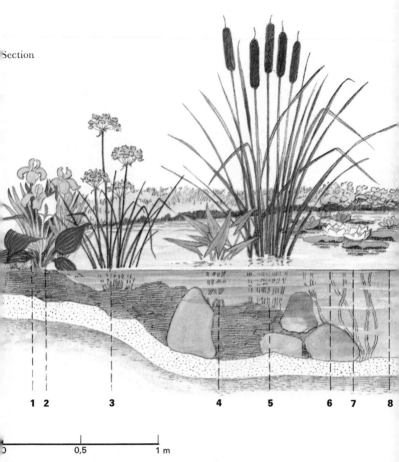

1 2   3   4   5   6 7   8

0   0,5   1 m

In making a water garden of whatever shape, the concrete or plastic base should provide different levels – so that each plant has the ideal depth of water for correct growth, which can vary from the damp soil at the margin to 40-50cm (15-20 in.). The depth of water should *never* exceed 50cm (20 in.) if children use the garden, because of the danger of drowning. Ideally the sides should be gently sloping and not vertical. The following water and bog-plants are illustrated here: *Iris pseudacorus* (**1**), *Calla palustris* (**2**), *Butomus umbellatus* (**3**), *Sagittaria sagittifolia* (**4**), *Typha angustifolia* (**5**), *Nymphaea* 'James Brydon' (**6**), *N. marliacea* 'Albida' and 'Chromatella' (**7-8**), *Caltha palustris* (**9**) and *Ranunculus lingua* (**10**).

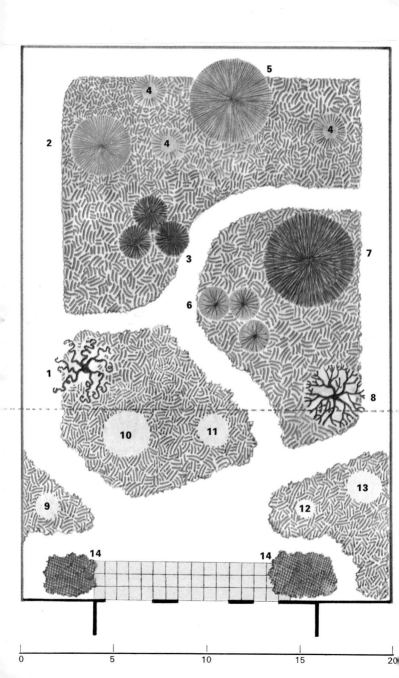

0   5   10   15   20

Many trees and bushes have very distinctive habits of growth. If you intend to specialise in this aspect of planting always remember to allow sufficient space for these beautifully shaped plants to develop fully. Also, allow for large, peaceful expanses of grass or low ground-cover plants to form the 'floor' of this exhibition of 'plant sculptures'. The following plants have been chosen for this example: *Corylus avellana* 'Contorta' (**1**), *Cryptomeria japonica* 'Lobbii' (**2**), *Juniperus communis* 'Hibernica' and 'Suecica' (**3-4**) underplanted with *J.c.* 'Repanda', *Chamaecyparis nootkatensis* 'Pendula' (**5**), *Picea glauca* 'Conica' (**6**), *Picea brewerana* (**7**), *Rhus typhina* 'Laciniata' (**8**), *Juniperus virginiana* 'Glauca' (**9**), *Chamaecyparis obtusa* 'Nana' (**10**), *Taxus baccata* 'Fastigiata' (**11**), *Juniperus media* 'Blaauw' (**12**), *Chamaecyparis pisifera* 'Filifera' (**13**) and *Buxus sempervirens* 'Bullata' (**14**) at bush height. The ground cover could be, *Cotoneaster dammeri* and *C. horizontalis*, *Asarum europaeum* and *Vinca minor*, all of which should form large, peaceful areas.

From the plan below one can see how it is possible to create a charming, and very special, garden of dwarf plants within a hexagonal framework. For centuries the Japanese and Chinese have made bonsai trees a speciality by growing tiny trees and bushes in beautiful pots and dishes of bronze and earthenware, keeping them dwarf with special techniques of pruning branches and roots. This miniature garden has been 'framed' with a 60-70cm (24-28 in.) tall, narrow, closely clipped hedge of, for example, *Ligustrum vulgare* 'Atrovirens', *Lonicera nitida* or box. The

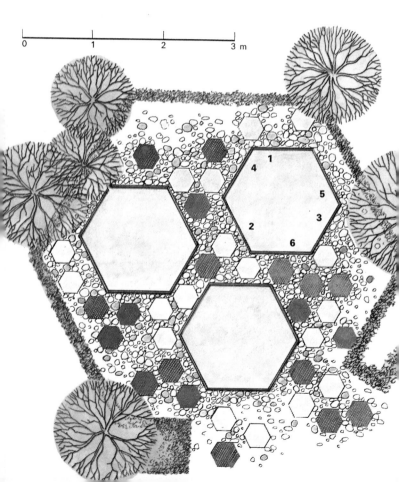

bushes shown outside the 'frame' should be of a light and graceful shape, e.g. *Cotoneaster salicifolius floccosus*. The three small beds of dwarf plants could be surrounded by planks of wood (which should be treated with a preservative other than creosote) and the ground covered with small pebbles amongst which some grey, brown and black hexagonal flagstones can be laid. In the bed shown above, three typical bonsai trees are shown: a dwarfed oak (**1**), a dwarf cypress (**2**), and a pine (**3**). To give added interest, some grasses and compact plants have been placed amongst the pebbles. Here, these are heather (**4**), small-leaved thyme (**5**) and fescue grass (**6**).

If specialising in ornamental grasses, a handsome, distinctive arrangement can be planted in a corner of the lawn. Illustrated below are egg-shaped 'islands' bordered by dark bricks with selected large, smooth cobbles covering the earth in order to produce a dramatic effect. This can be heightened by planting a couple of dark green yew bushes as a background. In this example *Taxus baccata*

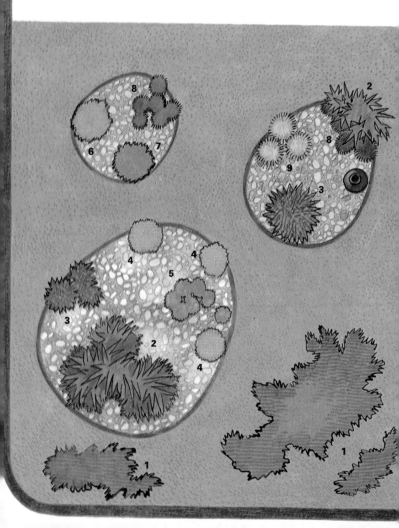

1) and the following grasses have been used: *Miscanthus sacchariflorus* (**2**), *M. inensis* 'Zebrinus' and 'Gracillimus' (**3-4**), *Bouteloua oligostachya* (**5**), *Carex grayi* **6**), *Pennisetum ruppelii* (**7**), *Festuca ovina* 'Glauca' (**8**) and *Avena sempervirens* (**9**).

1   2 m

If you wish to attract as many butterflies as possible to the garden, the simplest way is to plant bushes and perennials which are especially rich in nectar. The following, some of which are scented, are 'butterfly magnets': the Sumach tree, *Rhus typhina* 'Laciniata' (**1**), *Syringa prestoniae* 'Nocturne' (**2**), *Lavandula officinalis* (**3**), *Sedum spurium* 'Roseum' (**4**), *Echinops ritro* (**5**), *Aster amellus* 'King George' (**6**), *Thymus serpyllum* 'Splendens' (**7**), *Dianthus plumarius* 'Duchess of Fife' and 'Diamant' (**8-9**), *Buddleia davidii* 'Magnifica' and 'Royal Red' (**10-11**), *Liatris spicata* (**12**), *Solidago* 'Golden Wings' (**13**), *Scabiosa caucasica* (**14**), *Ligustrum vulgare* (**15**), *Salvia superba* 'East Friesland' (**16**), *Nepeta faassenii* (**17**) and *Sorbaria arborea* (**18**).

44 Tropical Lushness for Summer

The 'impatient' gardener can arrange a small corner with extremely fast-growing plants of almost tropical growth rates and which shoot up to an enormous size within a summer, but only live for just that one summer. Apart from several permanent plants, the following have been used: *Musa ensete* (**1**) (overwintered under glass), *Helianthus debilis* (**2**), *Kochia scoparia tricophylla* (**3**), *Nicotiana sanderae* (**4**), *Cucurbita pepo* (**5**), *Ricinus communis* (**6**), *Zea gigantea* 'Quadricolor' (**7**), and *Canna indica* 'R. Wallace' (**13**). The permanent plants, which ensure that this part of the garden does not stand empty during the winter, consist of the following: *Polygonatum multiflorum* (**8**), *Clematis sieboldii* (**9**), *Miscanthus sacchariflorus* (**10**), *Aristolochia durior* (**11**), *Avena sempervirens* (**12**), *Hosta fortunei* (**14**), *Heliopsis scabra* 'Patula' (**15**), *Helianthus salicifolius* (**16**), and a dark-leaved bush for the background, such as box or yew (**17**). The ground cover could be asarabacca. The bamboo fencing and wooden table, bench and 'paving' all contribute to the tropical effect.

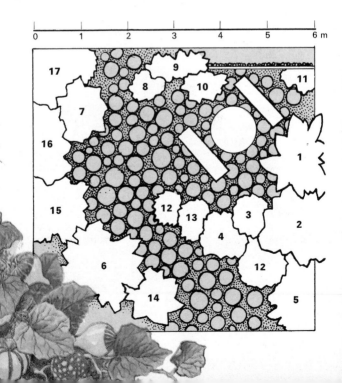

A bush clipped into a sphere or cube can produce a sharp contrast to free-growing bushes and trees. In earlier centuries, topiary work was used widely in formal gardens. Although some gardeners of today feel that it is unnatural to clip bushes into fine geometrical shapes, others see great beauty in the clean shapes of spheres, cylinders and pyramids and derive pleasure from forming these shapes from living green materials. In this example are the following bushes, all of which lend themselves to topiary work: *Buxus sempervirens* (**1**), *Lonicera pileata* (**2**), *Ligustrum vulgare* 'Atrovirens' (**3**), *Taxus media* 'Hicksii' (**4**), *Thuja occidentalis* 'Fastigiata' (**5**), *Taxus baccata* (**6**) and *Ribes alpinum* (**7**)

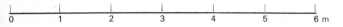

In a small, enclosed back yard one can easily create a foreign atmosphere by choosing plants which, for some reason, have an exotic appearance. The following have been used in this example: *Rhus typhina* 'Laciniata (**1**), *Rodgersia tabularis* (**2**), *Iris kaempferi* (**3**), *Miscanthus sacchariflorus* (**4**), *Yucca filamentosa* (**5**), *Potentilla fruticosa* 'Tangerine' (**6**), *Hypericum patulum* 'Hidcote' (**7**), *Sasa japonica* (**8**), *Actinidia kolomikta* (**9**), *Clematis* 'Jackmannii' (**10**), *Canna indica* and *Crinum powellii* (**11-12**) and *Ficus carica* (**13**).

Here is a small plot with plants chosen for their strong scent. They are: *Lonicera caprifolium* (**1**), *Hesperis matronalis* (**2**), *Sambucus nigra* (**3**), *Syringa vulgaris* 'Souvenir de Louis Spaeth' (**4**), *Lilium candidum* (**5**), *Lavandula officinalis* (**6**), lilies of the valley and violets (**7-8**), *Rosa rubiginosa* 'Lady Penzance' (**9**), *Cheiranthus cheiri* (**10**) and *Philadelphus* 'Avalanche' (**11**). Along the wall by the road a couple of Serbian firs (**12**), a couple of junipers (**13-14**) and a philadelphus (**15**) have been planted. Behind the back garden is a silver fir (**16**).

The following perennials and annuals have been used in the flower garden shown above: *Phlox paniculata* 'Excelsior' and 'Jules Sandeau' (**1-2**), *Ageratum houstonianum* and *Verbena venosa* among *Lilium regale* (**3-5**), *Aster amellus* 'King George' and *Salvia superba* 'East Friesland' (**6-7**), *Sedum spectabile* 'Brilliant' (**8**) and *Erigeron* 'Wuppertal' (**9**).

Yellow, Orange and Red

his contrasting garden is planted as follows: *Rudbeckia speciosa* (**1**), *Achillea*
ipendulina 'Coronation Gold' and *Solidago* 'Leraft' (**2-3**), *Salvia splendens* and
agetes erecta 'Yellow Supreme' (**4-5**), *Helenium* 'Moerheim Beauty' (**6**), and *H.*
he Bishop' (**7**).

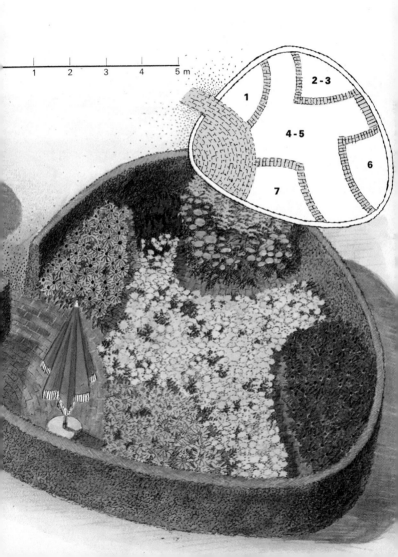

y the French windows one would have a splendid view of the whole garden from
he paved terrace. The garden appears bigger than it really is because of the tall
oven fencing panels placed at right angles to the boundary fences. Following the
ath around the garden brings one into the first 'room' – woodland flowers such as
lies and primulas (**6-11**). In the next 'room' one is greeted by brightly coloured
lue, yellow and red perennials like asters, *Chrysanthemum coccineum*, and helenium
13-15). There is a lovely soft light in the long, narrow path at the end of the
arden where one can plant ivy, asarabacca and periwinkle (**18-20**), which all
njoy shady positions. Next, in the last two rooms are hybrid tea roses (**23**) and
eat-loving plants such as rhododendrons and heathers (**24-30**). Further details of
he planting are given in the text description of this scheme (p. 203).

0	2	4	6	8	10 m

The garden is fenced and, where space permits, plants such as clematis, climbing roses and ivies form a peaceful background for the garden's main plants, rose and lilies.

It is suggested that the rosebeds in the lawn should be edged with dark bricks. The varieties of rose chosen are the clear yellow 'Peer Gynt' (**1**), the luminous red 'Super Star' (**2**), the coral red 'Fragrant Cloud' (**3**), the warm golden-yellow 'Whisky Mac' (**4**), the delicate pink 'Queen Elizabeth' (**5**), the pure white 'Iceberg' (**6**) and 'Pascali' (**7**), and the deep pink 'Pink Peace' (**8**). As ground cover between the roses, the evergreen *Cotoneaster dammeri* and *Vinca minor* could be used, among which early spring bulbs can grow. Here, summer plants such as *Ageratum houstonianum* 'Imperial Dwarf' and *Alyssum maritimum* 'Violet Queen' are also suitable.

The following varieties of lilies are grouped together in a corner of the garden near the patio: *Lilium martagon* (**9**), *L. hansonii* (**10**), *L.* 'Destiny' (**11**), *L. regale* (**12**), *L. speciosum* (**13**), *L. candidum* (**14**) and *L. tigrinum* (**15**). Alternatively, a choice can be made from the many modern hybrids available. Among many suitable ferns to use as ground cover one could try *Phyllitis scolopendrium* and *Polystichum aculeatum*.

The rest of the plants used in this garden should blend with the roses and lilies to produce a beautiful and harmonious picture. The following trees and bushes have been used: *Gleditsia triacanthos* 'Sunburst' (**16**), *Prunus subhirtella* 'Pendula Rubra' (**17**), *Cedrus deodara* (**18**), *Chamaecyparis pisifera* 'Filifera' (**19**), *Cryptomeria japonica* 'Lobbii' (**20**), *Viburnum fragrans* (**21**), *Daphne mezereum* (**22**), *Mahonia aquifolium* (**23**), *Magnolia stellata* (**24**), *Hypericum patulum* 'Hidcote' (**25**), *Viburnum burkwoodii* (**26**), *Cotoneaster salicifolius floccosus* (**27**), *Symphoricarpos albus* 'White Hedge' (**28**), *Ligustrum obtusifolium regelianum* (**29**), *Taxus baccata* (**30**) and *Hibiscus syriacus* (**31**), with *Cotoneaster dammeri* (**32**), *Hypericum calycinum* (**33**), *Lonicera bileata* (**34**) and *Vinca minor* (**35**) forming the ground cover between these.

| 0 | 3 | 6 | 9 m |

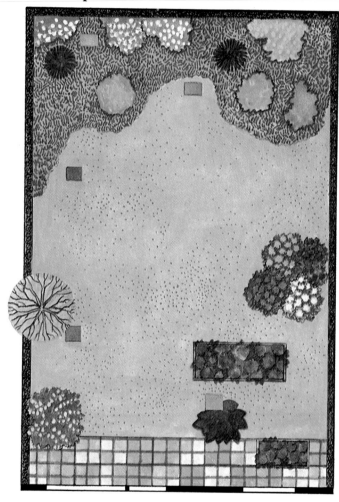

In paintings, pure bright colours such as red, yellow and blue will appear closer to the onlooker than the pale, delicate colours such as mauve, pale blue and pale pink. This effect can be used to advantage in a garden and thus create a greater feeling of size and depth by planting flowers according to 'colour perspective'. The sun-loving and brightly coloured flowers such as the red zonal pelargonium 'Zinck', the yellow *Tagetes patula* 'Sunny' and the blue *Ageratum*

houstonianum 'Imperial Dwarf' should be placed in the beds in the foreground; while shade-tolerant, delicately coloured flowers such as *Anemone hybrida* 'Queen Charlotte', *Astilbe arendsii* 'Cattleya', lily-of-the-valley and pale-toned foxgloves should be placed in scattered groups between dark, evergreen bushes in the background. The decorated, vertical posts in the illustration heighten the overall illusion and make the garden appear even larger from the terrace.

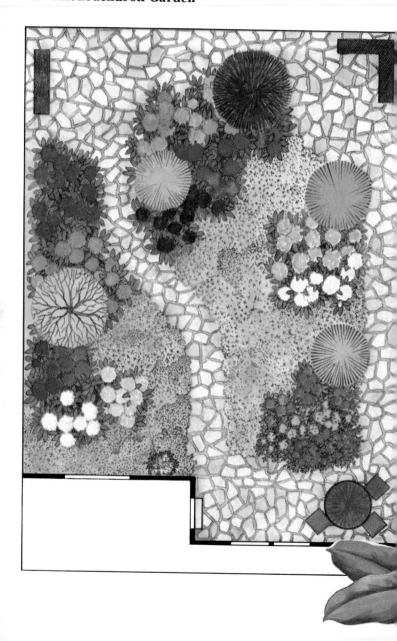

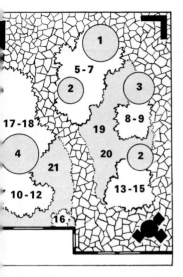

large-flowered evergreen and small-flowered deciduous species and hybrids look best when several plants are grouped together. They can also be associated with heathers and other low acid-loving plants.

In this example, apart from *Pinus parviflora* (**1**), *Juniperus virginiana* 'Canaertii' (**2**), *Cedrus atlantica* 'Glauca' (**3**) and *Magnolia soulangiana* (**4**), the following large-flowered species and varieties are used: *Rhododendron catawbiense* 'Grandiflorum', *R.* 'Countess of Athlone' and 'Purple Splendour' (**5-7**), *R. catawbiense* 'Album' and *R.* 'Pink Pearl' (**8-9**), *R. wardii*, *R.* 'Cunningham's White', and *R.* 'Hugh Koster' (**10-12**). There are also the following small-flowered species and varieties: *R. luteum*, *R.* 'Homebush' and 'Koster's Brilliant Red' (**13-15**), *Rhododendron ferrugineum*, *R. impeditum* 'Moerheimii' and *R. russatum* 'Cantabile' (**16-18**). Ground cover between the various groups consists of *Calluna vulgaris* and *Erica carnea* in several varieties, with *Hypericum calycinum* (**19-21**).

The rhododendron family with its great variety is one of the best to choose as a speciality. To achieve success, however, one must meet its relatively simple requirements, primarily an acid, peaty soil. Both the

0	2	4	6	8	10 m

Here a formal pool acts like a mirror for the surrounding trees, bushes and white summer clouds. The water surface must be kept clean and a narrow edge will form an attractive frame. The depth of the water need not be more than 20-30cm (8-12 in.). Along and near the edge of the pool, plants with outstanding foliage have been planted. They include the following trees and bushes: *Acer palmatum* 'Atropurpureum', Japanese maple, *Rhus typhina* 'Laciniata', sumach, and *Cotoneaster salicifolius floccosus*. Perennials which might be represented

are various silver grasses, a couple of hostas, *Asarum europaeum*, asara-bacca, *Bergenia cordifolia* 'Purpurea', elephant's ear, *Helianthus salici-folius*, willowleaf sunflower, *Iris pumila*, dwarf iris, *Laitris spicata*, gayfeather, *Polygonatum multiflorum*, Solomon's seal, and *Rodgersia tabularis*. The background should be as peaceful as possible and preferably consist of dark yew, *Taxus baccata*, just as the closely clipped 'theatrical wings' in the foreground of the example above should be of the same hedge plant.

For retired persons, the cultivation of espaliered fruit could be a fascinating hobby. This does not require great physical strength, but some specialised knowledge which can be acquired easily. The most important thing is to select the correct varieties and types. Some suitable varieties are: grape 'Black Hamburgh' (**1**), apple 'Golden Delicious' (**2**), and 'Merton Charm' (**3**), plum 'Kirke's Blue' (**4**), peach 'Peregrine' (**5**), pears 'Louise Bonne of Jersey' (**6**), 'Doyenné du Comice' (**7**) and 'Conference' (**8**), and apricot 'Early Moor Park' (**9**). On the left is a suggestion for training fruit trees against the walls and on espaliers in the garden.

0	1	2	3	4	5 m

Fruit and vegetables are steadily becoming more expensive to buy, and if space permits it is desirable to grow them in one's own garden. This plot has been planned to provide both fruit and vegetables in as decorative a way as possible. The area here has been devoted to the cherry 'Merton Glory' (**1**), peach 'Peregrine' (**2**), apple 'Golden Delicious' (**3**), plum 'Victoria' (**4**), apple 'Merton Charm' (**5**), apple 'James Grieve' (**6**), pear 'Conference' (**7**), pear 'Louise Bonne of Jersey' (**8**), red and black currants and gooseberries (**9**), onions, lettuce, spinach and various herbs (**10**).

0   2   4   6   8   10 m

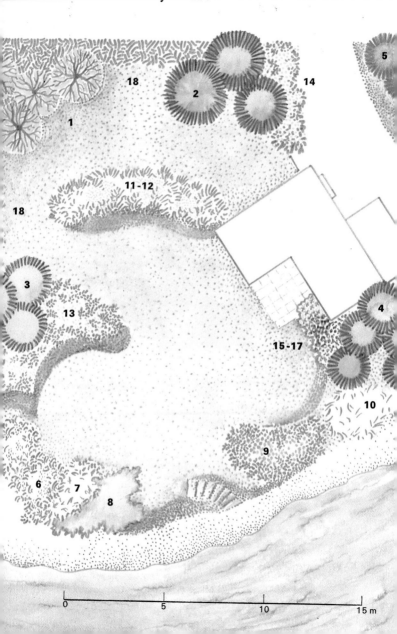

Plants for gardens near the sea should be chosen with great care as salt water is detrimental to many plants. However, there are many trees and shrubs which can tolerate sea spray. The following are illustrated in this example: *Sorbus intermedia* (**1**), *Pinus contorta* (**2**), *Picea sitchensis* (**3**), *Pinus mugo* (**4**), *Picea pungens* (**5**), *Hippophae rhamnoides* (**6**), *Elaeagnus commutata* (**7**), *Lycium chinense* (**8**), *Rosa rugosa* (**9**), *Salix repens* (**10**), *Berberis polyantha* and *Cytisus praecox* (**11-12**), *Rosa spinosissima* (**13**) and *R. hugonis* (**14**). Lavender, scarlet lychnis and loosestrife (**15-17**), all of which are perennials, enjoy the light soil near the terrace. Blackthorn forms the hedge (**18**). Various types of heather can be used to form the ground cover between the trees and bushes.

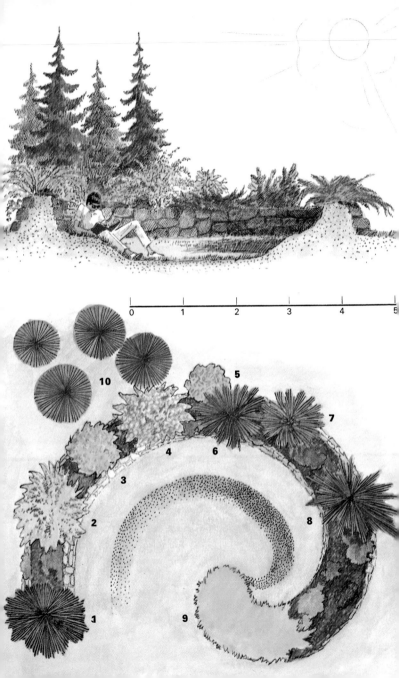

Shelter and reasonable privacy are sensible requirements for every garden, be it in the town or country. The example on the left shows how a warm 'sun-trap' can be arranged. The sides can be just a primitive mound or, as illustrated here, a stone wall planted with low shrubs. These are *Juniperus chinensis* 'Pfitzerana' (**1**), *Cytisus praecox* 'Allgold' (**2**), *Chaenomeles japonica* (**3**), *Cytisus scoparius* (**4**), *Cotoneaster horizontalis* (**5**), *Juniperus communis* 'Repanda' (**6**), *Pinus mugo* 'Pumilio' (**7**), *Juniperus squamata* 'Meyeri' (**8**), and *Stephanandra incisa* 'Crispa' (**9**). The ground cover between the bushes could be *Cotoneaster dammeri* and cushion-forming rock plants such as *Alyssum saxatile*, *Aubrieta intermedia* in various varieties and *Thymus serpyllum* 'Splendens'. A group of Serbian spruce (**10**) help to give even more shelter from the wind. If liked one could combine the stone wall with a low rockery facing the main garden. A cross-section of such an arrangement is illustrated below.

| 0 | | 1 | | 2 m |

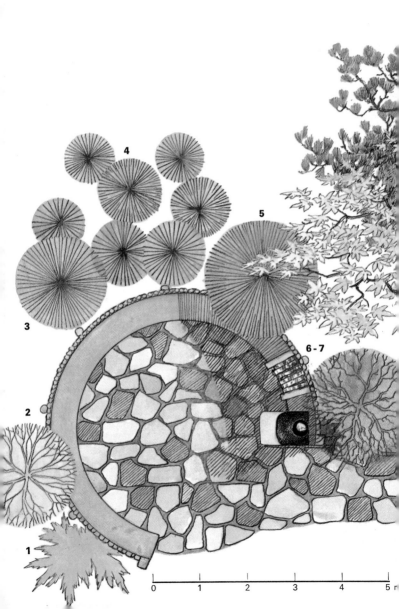

1

2

3

4

5

6 - 7

0   1   2   3   4   5 r

As summer evenings are often quite chilly, it would be useful to arrange a large, warm sitting-out area with an open fireplace. The area around this should be planned so that it harmonises with its surroundings, avoiding too much formality. The following trees and shrubs have been chosen for this example: *Juniperus chinensis* 'Pfitzerana' (**1**), *Acer ginnala* (**2**), *Pinus parviflora* (**3**), *Picea omorika* (**4**), *Pinus sylvestris* (**5**), *Quercus borealis* (**6**) and *Juniperus chinensis* 'Blaauw' (**7**).

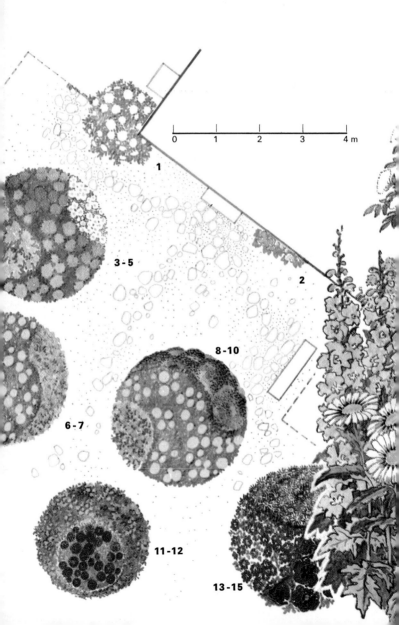

1

3 - 5

2

8 - 10

6 - 7

11 - 12

13 - 15

...ere circular beds cottagey flowers are used and allowed to merge and spread on to the surface of irregular stones and ...avel. The following could be used: an elderberry, *Sambucus* ...*rea*, or fragrant *Viburnum burkwoodii* (**1**), hollyhocks (**2**), ...onies, shasta daisy and delphiniums (**3-5**), lavender and the ...se 'Peace' (**6-7**), aubrieta, campanula and the rose 'Allgold' ...**-10**), periwinkle and the rose 'Hanne' (**11-12**), asters, ...iental poppies and perennial sunflowers (**13-15**).

For owners of a holiday house in moorland districts it is important to maintain and respect the landscape's original character, choosing garden plants which blend in with the natural vegetation. Examples of suitable plants are the smaller rhododendron species and the various types of heaths, *Calluna* and *Erica*, most types of broom, cytisus, and the juniper family with its numerous forms.

What was valid for the holiday house on the moor is also applicable to a house among mountains. One should respect their untouched and grandiose nature, and any gardening around the cabin should really contain plants which have not been 'improved'. Well suited to this purpose are *Campanula carpatica*, *Cyclamen europaeum* and *C. neapolitanum*, *Gentiana acaulis*, *Leontopodium alpinum* the edelweiss, and species of rhododendrons like *R. ferrugineum*.

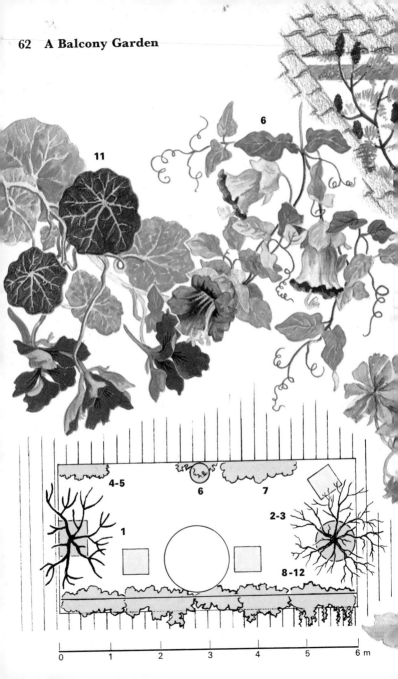

11

6

4-5

6

7

2-3

1

8-12

0   1   2   3   4   5   6 m

10

Today many modern houses have wide balconies or even flat roofs. They can be transformed into veritable 'hanging gardens' of lush vegetation especially if they face the sun. The plants can be grown in large containers. In this example the following plants have been used: *Rhus typhina* 'Laciniata' (**1**), *Betula pendula* 'Youngii' underplanted with *Hypericum calycinum* (**2-3**), *Jasminum nudiflorum* underplanted with *Potentilla fruticosa* 'Jackman's Variety' (**4-5**), *Cobaea scandens* (**6**), *Pelargonium zonale* 'Zinck' (**7**) (which can replace tall, late flowering tulips), white, pink and purple petunias, *Pelargonium peltatum* 'Mme. Crousse', *Tropaeolum lobbianum* the climbing nasturtium, and *Lysimachia nummularia* or creeping Jenny (**8-12**).

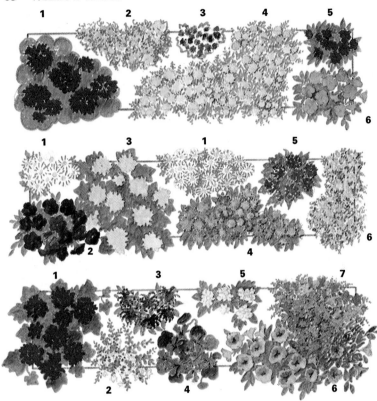

For window box arrangements the flowers should complement each other in the same manner as those in a garden. At the most there should be five to seven different kinds per box, according to size.

Scheme 1—*Pelargonium zonale* 'Zinck' (**1**), *Lobelia* 'Hamburgia' (**2**), *Verbena venosa* (**3**), *Tagetes patula* 'Petite Yellow' (**4**), *Salvia splendens* 'Scarlet Fire' (**5** and *Petunia* 'Sugar Plum' (**6**).

Scheme 2—*Chrysanthemum frutescens* (**1**), *Petunia* 'Purple Plum' (**2**), *Pelargonium peltatum* 'Mme. Crousse' (**3**), *Ageratum houstonianum* 'Imperial Dwarf' (**4**), *Begonia semperflorens* 'Danica Scarlet' (**5**) and *Alyssum maritimum* 'Violet Queen' (**6**).

Scheme 3—*Pelargonium peltatum* 'L'Elegante' (**1**), *Lysimachia nummularia* (**2**), *Heliotropium* 'Marina' (**3**), nasturtium 'Whirlybird Scarlet' (**4**) *Calceolaria integrifolia* (**5**), *Petunia* 'Sugar Plum' (**6**) and *Tagetes patula* 'Marietta' (**7**).

Scheme 1

Scheme 2

Scheme 3

Pots, boxes and tubs with beautiful groups of summer flowers have become popular in many gardens, where they are placed on terraces or on patios to provide a summer-long focus of colour. When planting out it is often wise not to mix too many different types of flowers in the containers. The red clay pot shown above is planted solely with mixed climbing nasturtiums (**1**), the vase of imitation stone with trailing *Lobelia* 'Hamburgia' (**2**), and the arrangement in the cement box comprises *Chrysanthemum frutescens*, *Lysimachia nummularia* and *Viola cornuta* (**3-5**). The wooden tub is planted with *Pelargonium peltatum* 'Achievement' and *Petunia* 'Sugar Plum' (**6-7**). The asbestos-cement window box is full of the low, early-flowering tulip 'Bellona' (**8**) which can be replaced later by profuse flowering *Tagetes* varieties such as 'Petite Yellow' and 'Sunny'.

PLANNING YOUR GARDEN

The first steps in creating a garden may involve levelling of the site, addition of topsoil, laying of flagstones and paths, planting of hedges and erection of fences. After these tasks have been completed, one can then start choosing plants. It is at the final stage of actually planting where problems often begin. The choice of trees, bushes, perennials, annuals, bulbs and tubers is so vast that it is often difficult to choose the relatively small number for which there will be room in the average garden. Yet in addition to this, once one has selected the plants one likes, the problem arises as to how they should be arranged to best advantage and to be able to develop freely without cramping each other. One ought therefore to seek as much information as possible about potential plants, both by seeing them actually growing in gardens open to the public and as illustrated in reference books.

It is a particularly important matter with trees and shrubs, as they will remain in the same position for many years, and one must visualise how tall and wide these plants will be in 10 or 15 years' time. It is also important to know their habits of growth. Finally, one must remember to check on their special requirements with regard to soil, sun, shade and other conditions.

* * * * *

The numbered sections that follow are intended to amplify the text which accompanies the plates, and so the numbers in each heading also refer to the corresponding colour plates.

1 The Shapes of Trees

As can be seen from Plate 1, trees have many habits of growth. There are, for example, pyramidal and pillar-shaped trees such as fir, poplar and thuja – represented here by *Picea omorika*, Serbian spruce, *Picea pungens*, blue fir, *Populus nigra* 'Italica',

145

Lombardy poplar, and *Thuja occidentalis* 'Fastigiata'. All have a characteristic upright form. Then, in contrast there are large, broad-crowned trees such as oak, elm, lime and fir – which are represented here by *Quercus robur*, common oak, with its picturesque gnarled branches, which can also be seen on *Juglans regia*, walnut, and *Robinia pseudoacacia*, false acacia. *Ulmus glabra*, the wych elm, has a slightly drooping fan-shaped crown; *Tilia platyphylla*, the broad-leafed lime, a regular crown (the shape of which reminds one of the heart-shaped lime leaf) and *Pinus sylvestris*, the Scots pine, carries a broad, irregular crown on a tall, slim, reddish trunk. These are trees with beautiful habits of growth, but also trees which are greedy and create a great deal of shadow, and should therefore not be used in the average garden. The same applies to popular trees such as *Aesculus hippocastanum*, the horsechestnut, and *Fagus sylvatica* 'Purpurea', the purple beech. Finally there are trees with a decidedly weeping habit such as *Betula pendula* 'Tristis', the Swedish birch, *Fagus sylvatica* 'Pendula', the weeping beech, and *Salix chrysocoma*, the weeping willow.

Maintaining the proper scale
Although with the help of secateurs and saw one can keep most trees within bounds, such heavy pruning almost always spoils their natural shape and beauty. Thus for smaller gardens it is advisable only to choose trees that are naturally of moderate growth. There is a wide choice of such trees with the same variations in growth habits – tall, conical, dome-shaped or weeping – as have been illustrated in the plates. Of course, in the small garden of a terrace house there will be room for only one or two small trees.

Choosing specimen trees
When choosing trees at a nursery it is often best to select ones which are not too regular in shape. Trees with slightly gnarled trunks will, for example, look much more attractive near the walls of the house, and such trees planted in a group will be more picturesque than a group of completely uniform, perfectly shaped specimens. In choosing trees to be planted near the house one should also pay attention to the material of the building so that the colour of the flowers, and sometimes the leaves, will not clash.

For example, a Japanese cherry tree with its delicate, pale pink flowers would be most unfortunate near a house of new, red bricks. As a rule, pine trees always look attractive when planted near a wall, and Serbian and blue spruces are always pleasing on a lawn in front of any type of house.

Trees individually and in groups

In contrast to the broad-crowned deciduous trees which are easier to place, slim evergreens have an architectural air about them which can easily be too dominating when planted singly. The pyramidal and pillar-shaped conifers are essentially solitary plants and as such should be planted so they can develop naturally – say, in the lawn or in wide open areas of ground-cover plants, so that the trees can be seen from all angles. They are most effective in groups of 3–5 or so, but never so many that they lose their character. Groups of trees can be beautiful, but the individual tree is just as notable, because a tree develops the finest proportions when planted in the open.

2   The Shapes of Shrubs

As can be seen from the examples in Plate 2, shrubs also have many different habits of growth. Some, for example *Rosa rugosa*, have a reasonably tall, broad, close, twiggy growth while others like *Juniperus communis* 'Repanda', *Cotoneaster dammeri* and *C.horizontalis*, and *Hypericum calycinum*, have low, spreading or creeping growth. *Rosa hugonis* has a tall, broad, slightly drooping habit in contrast to *Syringa vulgaris*, the lilac, which has a compact, rather upright habit. Two other contrasting habits are those of *Corylus avellana* 'Contorta', the corkscrew hazel, which has a peculiar twisted and gnarled form, and *Picea glauca* 'Conica', with very regular, pyramid-shaped growth. Finally *Chaenomeles japonica*, the small Japanese quince, has a low, spreading and slightly weeping habit.

Differing growth habits

In general, bushes which shoot out from the root and have a broad, compact, twiggy growth such as *Rosa rugosa*, or *Symphoricarpos albus* the snowberry, will be well suited for use as a broad, close hedge or thicket for a holiday house garden or a small front garden facing the road. On the other hand, the lower growing types will cover large slopes, or can be used as a ground cover between tall trees. Bushes of tall, broad, slightly weeping habit, such as *Rosa hugonis* and *R*. 'Nevada', should always have room to develop naturally and to a certain extent the same is true of various other flowering shrubs, for example *Cotoneaster salicifolius floccosus*, *Cytisus praecox*, *Deutzia rosea* 'Carminea', *Kolkwitzia amabilis*, *Spiraea arguta* and *Weigela hybrida*. Many conifers also need sufficient room on all sides to show off their distinguished beauty, such as *Chamaecyparis pisifera* 'Filifera' and 'Squarrosa', and *Juniperus media* 'Pfitzerana'. Bushes of this type should either be placed in the lawn or be underplanted with low ground cover bushes such as *Cotoneaster dammeri*, *Hypericum calycinum* or *Juniperus horizontalis*.

Shrubberies with matching types of bush
If one wishes to have several different bushes in a shrubbery, designed say for privacy, then one should choose bushes with similar habits and height. For example, the following shrubs would be most suitable when planted together: *Forsythia intermedia*, *Kolkwitzia amabilis*, *Ribes sanguineum* and *Spiraea vanhouttei*. However, the whole effect would be ruined by the introduction of, say, *Potentilla fruticosa*. To start with, there would be a large gap in the shrubbery because the potentilla is not particularly large and later on it would become quite swamped by the neighbouring shrubs. One can, however, use small shrubs at the front of the shrubbery with good effect.

How close to plant?
How closely together shrubs are planted depends entirely on their purpose. In a mixed planting of larger shrubs 1½–2m (about 5–6½ft) should be allowed between the plants, but only 1½m (5ft) if a hedge is to be formed. If one type of shrub is to be used as a free-growing hedge, then the distance between the plants should only be about 75cm (2½ft). However, should the bushes be used as solitary plants planted in the open, with low ground cover, then they should be at least 2½–4m (7–13ft) apart. The distance between shrubs of one kind should be 1–1½m (3–5ft) if they are

to be planted in groups of 3–5 or more, for they will then grow together as an entity.

3 The Shapes of Perennials

As can be seen from Plate 3, the growth habit of perennials is just as varied as that of trees and bushes. Some perennials such as *Miscanthus sacchariflorus*, elephant grass, *Verbascum olympicum*, great mullein, *Eremurus robustus*, desert candle, *Yucca filamentosa* and kniphofias (or red hot pokers) have a distinguished and very decorative shape. Perennials of this type should be allowed to stand freely – for example in the foreground of a herbaceous border – or in among flagstones where gaps have been left for individual plantings. Alternatively, they can be planted in a large rock garden and underplanted with spreading shrubs such as *Cotoneaster dammeri* or low cushion plants such as *Saxifraga* 'Peter Pan' and *Thymus serpyllum* 'Splendens'. They are displayed to the best advantage against a peaceful, dark green background of evergreen shrubs. Other perennials such as michaelmas daisies, erigerons, phloxes, heleniums and *Rudbeckia speciosa*, which form broad, close clusters of flowers, can be used to advantage in flowerbeds with annuals, bulbs and tuberous plants to form an attractive colour scheme.

Spacing perennials

The planting distance between perennials varies widely. For example, with *Eremurus robustus*, the foxtail lily, only one plant should be used per square metre (about 11 sq. ft). To plant too closely means that plants become crowded and their appearance is spoiled; they will also compete excessively for food and moisture supplies. Generally speaking, this is also true of annuals, bulbs and tuberous plants. Any good book on cultivation will give advice on the correct spacing.

4 The Colours and Shapes of Leaves

As a rule, green is the most dominant colour in a garden. Just think of the lawn which is, without doubt, one of the most important elements in creating a peaceful and pleasant picture.

However, the other plants' various shades of green leaves all contribute to the scene.

Cold and warm leaf colours

Plate 4 shows examples of how different green leaves can be in their colour and shape. As can be seen, leaves vary from the palest green found in the young vine, *Vitis vinifera*, through the strong lush green of *Iris germanica*, to the almost sombre dark green of box, *Buxus sempervirens*, yew, *Taxus baccata* and ivy, *Hedera helix*. Green also spans the colder blue and grey–green shades of silver fir, *Picea pungens* 'Koster', white poplar, *Populus alba*, grey poplar, *P.canescens*, silver berry, *Elaeagnus commutata* and blue fescue grass, *Festuca glauca*, the names of which clearly indicate the colour of leaf.

It is not uncommon to see gardens arranged with the pure, lush greens and the cold, blue–greens in disharmony with each other. It is wiser to keep these two shades of green apart.

If one planted a fresh green bamboo, *Sinarundinaria murielae*, beside a blue–green Atlas cedar, *Cedrus atlantica* 'Glauca', the two plants would clash both in colour and shape. The pale green bamboo leaves and the whole plant's graceful habit of growth would be more apparent in the company of other plants with fresh green leaves, such as the elegant willow-leafed sunflower *Helianthus salicifolius* and the fescue grass *Festuca glauca*. The blue–green Atlas cedar needs quite different neighbours if it is to look its best. This handsome tree would look more effective planted near broad, blue–green juniper bushes, say *Juniperus media* 'Pfitzerana glauca', blue fescue grass, masses of carnations and other perennials, such as the sea holly *Eryngium amethystinum*, and *Gypsophila paniculata*.

Autumn shades

The autumn or fall colours of brown, yellow and red are so rich and varied that they almost appear as a second blooming, and one should certainly take them into consideration when planning the garden. Neither the autumn red of *Berberis thunbergii*, nor the perhaps even richer colour of *Cotoneaster acutifolius* should be missing. The wonderful golden red of *Amelanchier laevis*, which also has scented white flowers in the spring, must be included, if for that reason alone. The golden shades can be found in *Cerci-diphyllum japonicum*, similar to the Judas tree, and *Ginkgo biloba*, the maidenhair tree. Rainy weather is not good for producing autumn shades as sunshine is really needed to enhance the splendid colours. Not all trees and bushes change colour in the autumn. Lilac leaves, for example, fall when still green and most fruit trees lose their leaves when they are dark brown and shabby. Evergreen trees and shrubs seldom have autumn shades, but many of them take on a brown or yellowish tinge in the winter, to become quite green again next spring.

Autumn colours are not limited to trees and shrubs. Many climbing plants and perennials turn yellow, orange or red before they lie dormant. Just think of the Virginia creeper's lovely red leaves or the large golden leaves of *Hosta glauca*.

Other leaf-colours
Not all plants have green leaves. Some trees and shrubs have red or yellow leaves even from early spring. Such subjects should be used with caution as their unusual colours do not always blend with the other plants in an ordinary garden. For example trees and bushes with red or yellow leaves could be most unfortunate against red or yellow brick walls. There are exceptions which could be used in a lawn or between evergreen shrubs, as for example red-leaved subjects such as *Acer palmatum* 'Atropurpureum', Japanese maple, *Berberis thunbergii* 'Atropurpurea', *Cotinus coggygria* 'Royal Purple', smoke tree, *Fagus sylvatica* 'Purpurea', copper beech, and *Prunus cerasifera* 'Atropurpurea', purple plum, and yellow-leaved shrubs like *Acer palmatum* 'Aureum', another Japanese maple, *Cornus alba* 'Spaethii', dogwood, and *Sambucus nigra* 'Aurea', golden elder.

Seasonal variations of a lawn
The lawn probably gives the widest variation in colour. Without doubt the gardener's ideal is a uniform green over the whole area. The less perfect lawn with its patches of moss, daisies, speedwell and even dry areas is, in fact, far richer. The gardener should learn to see the lawn as a living part of the garden which changes its appearance according to the season, as do the rest of the garden's plants. After all, we find it quite natural that clouds dis-

appear when the sky is overcast, that colours change from morning till evening and that autumn produces wonderful colours on everything green.

The shapes of leaves
The shape as well as the colour of a leaf is important when arranging plants. If several types of plant are to form a harmonious group it is often best to choose plants with similar shaped leaves. This has been suggested in Plate 10. Other plants with striking foliage include *Rhus typhina* 'Laciniata', sumach, *Magnolia tripetala* and *Liriodendron tulipifera*, tulip tree. One might keep one part of the garden for trees and shrubs with particularly ornamental leaves and in this way create a section of exceptional beauty.

5–6 The Warm and Cold Colours of Flowers

As mentioned elsewhere in the book, it is fairly easy to arrange plants according to the colour of their leaves. It is far more difficult when it comes to flowers as colour sense is a very personal thing. Some people are very sensitive to bright colours and strong contrasts, while others are not disturbed in the slightest by colour clashes. However, it is always useful to have some guide lines when planning.

Yellow, orange and red are 'warm' colours. They are found in calendulas, evening primroses (*Oenothera*), geums, perennial sunflowers (*Helianthus* and *Heleniums*), most French and African marigolds (*Tagetes*), mulleins (*Verbascum*), primroses, many pansies such as 'Helios', zonal pelargoniums such as 'Orange Bob', nasturtiums, and many varieties of oriental poppy (*Papaver orientalis*). Reddish–purple shades found for example in the michaelmas daisy *Aster novi-belgii* 'Lady France', many phloxes, and peonies such as 'Rubra plena', form the transition between the 'warm' and the 'cold' colours.

Blue, violet, pink and white as well as yellowish–greens and grey are 'cold' colours. These colours can be found in *Centaurea montana* 'Grandiflora', and annual cornflowers, most delphiniums, globe thistles (echinops), *Lilium regale*, lily-of-the-valley, *Clematis* 'Lasurstern', *Iris germanica* 'Braithwaite', *Aster frikartii* 'Wonder of Stafa' and *Aster amellus* 'King George', *Campanula carpatica* and *Gentiana acaulis*. Flowers within this group of colours do not always complement the 'warm' colours. Exceptions are the bluer shades of purple and mauve, which can be used equally well amongst pink and blue or yellow and orange flowers.

Blending with the surroundings
As a rule, flowers of 'warm' and 'cold' colours do not look well together. Yellowish red and yellow–green are typical examples of this and should be kept apart both in bunches and beds of flowers.

Plants with flowers within the cold colour range should be planted in shady positions between conifers or other evergreens, so that the feeling of coolness is emphasised. Flowers within the warm colour range should, however, be planted in a sunny position where the surroundings are so brightly illuminated that they can compete with the intense colours.

7 Flowers in Shade and Sunlight

Even if the gardener has little knowledge of colour harmonies, nature helps by softening the worst clashes with green leaves. Practically speaking, most flowers appear pleasing together provided plants are kept in surroundings which would be natural to them. The trouble starts when plants which do not normally grow together are thus placed. The position of plants in the garden can be determined by their natural habitat, as suggested in Plate 7.

Not all sun-loving plants complement each other, so one should pay attention to their different natural habits and always keep them separated. For example, in a meadow one can find the strong yellow, blue and red of marsh marigold, forget-me-nots and campion, while on the sunny heath one finds the same strong colours, in, for example, tormentil, marsh gentian and rosebay willowherb.

8 Colour Contrasts and Colour Harmonies

There are certain general rules with regard to blending and clashing colours. For example it would be unfortunate to plant a group of rhododendrons consisting only of orange–red, purple–red and pinkish–red varieties which, placed close together, would have a most unharmonious effect. Red geraniums among reddish–pink roses, or a delicate pink Japanese cherry close to a new brick wall, would be just as much of an eyesore.

Although variety is the very essence of life, uniformity can provide a peaceful harmony. Colour contrasts help to give the variety – for example, yellow tulips between blue scillas or blue monkshood between yellow goldenrod. Uniformity comes from working within the same colour range – for example, pale yellow, dark yellow, orange–yellow and brownish yellow.

Evergreens for good colour contrasts
If one wants the colour of a certain plant to feature prominently it is necessary to think carefully about the colours of the plants which will appear behind and around it. It is all too easy for the distinctive flower not to stand out. The examples given on the left hand side of Plate 8 illustrate the importance of the correct colour associations.

The colours of most flowers will blend with green, especially with evergreens which are often quite dark, e.g. box and yew, both most effective backgrounds. A yew hedge as a background for a flower garden is an excellent idea, as is also a flowering fruit tree in front of a large group of firs or pines. Then the white or pale pink flowers of the fruit tree stand out clearly, whereas they would be lost when viewed against a pale sky.

Complementary colours
Whenever people look at a colour, they subconsciously wish to see its *complementary colour*, i.e. the colour which appears opposite to it in a colour circle. If one arranges in a circle, the colours red, yellow, green, blue and purple, together with their respective intermediates, one discovers that opposite red is bluish green, opposite yellow is violet, opposite green is purplish–red and opposite blue is reddish–orange. It is widely accepted that these complementary, or contrasting colours as they are sometimes called, have a pleasing effect together. However, it would be a bit much to base all the colour harmonies in a garden entirely upon contrasting colours. Usually one works within the same colour

range for most of the plants in any self-contained area, and thus ends up with a predominantly red, yellow or blue garden in which one arranges the odd plant with flowers of a contrasting colour. One could, for example, imagine a blue garden with the odd yellow *Potentilla fruticosa* which would emphasise all the blues and so would bring the garden to life.

If one is in doubt about the complementary colour of a certain flower, one needs only to stare at it for a minute and then close one's eyes (or hold one's hands over them if the sun is bright). The complementary colour is then seen as an after-image on the retina.

Colour arrangements

An arrangement confined just to the warm shades of orange and red can be extremely effective, as is demonstrated in the example on the right hand page of Plate 8. Pleasing effects can also be created using shades of other colours, for example the blues, purples and pinks of *Aster amellus*, delphiniums, erigerons, *Salvia superba* and *Sedum spectabile*. A particularly outstanding effect is achieved with the shades of pink, purple–red and purple varieties of *Ageratum houstonianum*, *Aster novibelgii*, *Gypsophila repens*, phloxes and *Verbena venosa*.

Red is an extremely dominant colour and one should think carefully before using it. However, it is excellent when used correctly to emphasise and to best effect – it gives the finishing touch. Red should be used with discretion in the garden, for example *Lychnis chalcedonica* and red geraniums should only be used to show up the other colours. They are not attractive in large groups and clash unpleasantly with most other reds. Yet, attractive colour contrasts can be produced if large areas of flowers in bright red, for example *Salvia splendens* 'Blaze of Fire', are placed close to large areas of, for example, *Tagetes patula* 'Petite Yellow' and shining blue *Lobelia pumila* 'Crystal Palace'. The strength of colour is tremendous, but as all three colours are equally strong, it is very effective.

9 Pretty Posies

When it comes to planting herbaceous borders, it is helpful to pick a bunch of the flowers concerned. If the colours concerned blend well together, then one can be certain that this will also be the effect in the border. The examples shown in Plate 9 illustrate two such harmonious posies and beds. There is an enormous number of perennials to choose from, so that many different 'posies' can be made. However, one must always remember to take the flowering season into consideration. It would be a pleasure to behold a bunch of *Gypsophila paniculata* 'Bristol Fairy' with the white regal lily, *Lilium regale*, the white everlasting *Anaphalis yedoensis* and the lilac–red *Salvia superba* 'East Friesland'. Again, one might match the goldenrod *Solidago* 'Leraft' with the orange–red rose 'Korona' or indeed the same goldenrod with a couple of bright red dahlias and possibly a sunflower or two. Both arrangements produce an excellent effect either as a bouquet or in the garden. Finally, one could make a bouquet of the pale pink peony, *Peonia lactiflora* 'Mikado', with a couple of stems from the pale pink shrub *Kolkwitzia amabilis*.

10–13 Attractive Schemes

The plants used to illustrate the harmonious arrangements shown on Plates 10–13 have been chosen with careful consideration. By 'harmony' one implies that a certain law and order exists among the different parts of the assembled entity. In selecting plants for the examples, attention was paid to every single plant's habit of growth, height, breadth, leaf shape and colour, colour of flower, and the plant's special requirements with regard to soil, sun, shade and other so-called growth factors. Several examples can be seen in the plan around any tree, be it a well-shaped conifer or a moderate-sized deciduous tree with beautiful flowers. Shrubs, perennials, bulbs and tubers have been selected so that their individual shape and colour will enhance the particular trees. Finally, it must be emphasised how important it is to give the whole planting scheme an attractive ground cover (as a rule in the form of a peaceful green area of ground cover plants) and to create a good background for particularly well-shaped plants, for example tulips and lilies. Each plant shown in these plates has a definite part to play.

If the several types of plant are to form a group, then a well-balanced effect can be achieved by the use of plants with similar leaves as shown in Plate 10. It is often wise to let one or two larger shrubs or trees be the dominant plants – the 'soloists' – and let the others complete the picture as in Plate 11. Such trees can simply 'perform' in front of a dark background if they are pale-flowered (as on Plate 12), but where several distinctive trees are used, then they must be placed relatively far apart to allow them space both to develop freely and to produce their individual effects (Plate 13).

Natural law and order

A balanced arrangement is usually based on a certain natural battle between the plants, but this is a fight which is to the advantage of the gardener! A low ground cover plant such as *Vinca minor*, the lesser periwinkle, should be surrounded by others which are strong enough to keep it in check, but which on the other hand will not spread out over it. The large-leaved *Hosta fortunei* keeps within certain bounds, but will not allow the vinca to creep in under its large, shady leaves. In this way it is an ideal natural limit. Large shrubs, which are often rather bare at the base. should be underplanted with low bushes so that the grass does not intrude under the larger bushes. It is often preferable to have a natural transition rather than a grass edge which needs constant trimming and attention.

One should not plant rock plants at random either; instead, see that the more vigorous plants are kept in check by small bushes or evergreens and that the weaker plants are grouped together otherwise they will be swamped. Harmony is not just based upon peace and quiet, but also on a well thought-out plan by which the plants keep each other in check: there should be a natural interplay between the vigorous and weak growing varieties.

Use of individual plants

A harmonious arrangement of plants has the variety of tall and short and the differences between large areas and individual free-growing plants. A tree with a well-formed crown and an attractive trunk should stand among low plants or quite openly in the lawn, which is itself a form of ground cover. Many trees, both larger and smaller, must be considered as individualists and should always stand alone. Examples might be *Cedrus atlantica* 'Glauca', Atlas cedar, *Picea brewerana*, weeping spruce, *Picea glauca* 'Conica', dwarf spruce, *Pinus griffithi*, Himalayan pine, and *Sciadopitys verticillata*, umbrella pine. In a garden, one could not really imagine planting any of these in large numbers; it is as though they were created to stand alone.

It is not only trees which can be 'soloists'; this can also apply to shrubs such as *Buddleia davidii*, *Cotoneaster salicifolius floccosus*, *Enkianthus campanulatus*, the pagoda bush, *Kolkwitzia amabilis*, and *Syringa chinensis*, the Rouen lilac. Many perennials too look out of place in beds amongst other tall herbaceous plants, and need to be admired from 'top to toe' for best effect. Examples are *Aruncus silvester*, goat's-beard. *Eremurus robustus*, foxtail lily, kniphofias, or red hot pokers such as 'Fireflame', *Miscanthus sacchariflorus*, elephant grass, and *Yucca filamentosa*, adam's needle.

The beauty of summer and winter
The shapes of leaves are so varied and dominant that one could plant a garden to achieve contrasts between rough and smooth, or heavy and light. Contrasts are excellent not only in colours, buy also in shapes. Think how pleasant it is to see trees such as *Ailanthus altissima*, the tree of heaven, *Aralia elata*, the Japanese angelica tree, *Enkianthus campanulatus*, the pagoda bush, *Liriodendron tulipifera*, the tulip tree and *Rhus typhina* 'Laciniata', sumach. However, one should also think of the winter outline of trees and shrubs, with their naked branches etched against the pale sky or against snow. Then such distinctive forms as *Salix matsudana tortuosa*, the corkscrew willow, or the ordinary laburnums with their Japanese-art outlines, really come into their own.

Planning for harmony
A harmonious arrangement of plants will not necessarily be attractive when newly planted, but will evolve year by year, provided sufficient room has been allowed for the plants to develop. One day, possibly after 10–15 years' growth, these trees and shrubs will have become too large in contrast to the other plants. Then it will be necessary to make the decision to cut them

back, perhaps removing some shrubs altogether, and often reconsidering the entire garden plan.

14-15 Planning the Front Garden

A front garden should enhance the house, and if possible it should also take into consideration the overall picture of the road. This may only be possible on modern housing estates where the house frontage is common property. Such open gardening is usually planned by the developers. but it can often be developed by residents acting together. Of course, in such cases any local by-laws should be taken into account. The plan should be as simple as possible, with the use of only a few types of plants.

Grass can be considered as a low, evergreen ground cover, but it can be annoying to cut grass between trees and bushes and the the lawn could be substituted by ground-cover planting. The following plants are most suitable as low ground cover for the front garden: *Cotoneaster hybridus* 'Skogholm' or 'Pendulus', *Stephanandra incisa* and *Symphoricarpos chenaultii* 'Hancock'. Once the bushes have covered the ground, there is no more work, as weeds will not be troublesome. Really low ground-cover plants such as the completely evergreen *Cotoneaster dammeri*, *Vinca minor* or *Waldsteinia ternata* could also be used.

Closing off the back garden

The front garden is often open to the back garden on both sides, but one ought to close one way. In Plates 14 and 15 this has been done with the help of the garage which extends from the house to the boundary. This could also be done using a larchlap or inter-woven fence, a close arrangement of plants or by building a stone wall. The old-fashioned idea of being able to 'walk around the house' ruins any chance of privacy in the garden.

Low fences

One can limit the front garden by use of a low kerb of granite or cement, or a row of cobbles – but not a row of boulders, which would look like a set of false teeth! The kerbstone is only 5–10cm (2–4in) higher than the level of the pavement, but if one prefers a more fenced protection, one could build a stone or brick wall, limiting the height to 50–75cm ($1\frac{1}{2}$–$2\frac{1}{2}$ft) for best effect. A double wall with plants in soil between the two sides can be very effective: it should be sufficiently broad to ensure that the earth core does not dry out too quickly and that there is enough room for an attractive arrangement of plants.

16   Plants against a Wooden Fence

Nearly all types of fence are a blot on the landscape until they have had plants near them, but this should not deter one from using larchlap or interwoven fences as a boundary or to divide up the garden, because they are particularly space-saving. One must remember that the wind must be able to move air between the slats of the fence. An airtight fence gives little effective shelter since wind creates miniature whirlwinds at ground level on the leeward side. The greatest shelter is produced when the space between the slats forms 30% of the total area of the fence. These gaps between the slats are also advantageous for climbing plants which they can weave in and out to achieve a good anchorage. Climbing plants always need to be well attached to whatever 'frame' they grow upon, otherwise their stems can be damaged in stormy weather. Many clematis which seem to die for no apparent reason are in fact victims of unsuspected wind damage.

Woodland conditions for climbing plants
A wooden fence is an excellent place for climbing plants as they grow most naturally in woods where the roots are in damp soil. rich in humus, with the lower parts of the plants in the shade and the flowers at the top seeking the sun. The soil should be treated with compost and peat near the wooden fence. Many climbers will prefer the shady side of a fence, although this will not always be practical; if not, it may be possible to shade the roots with another plant.

'Climbing' roses are in fact not true climbers, but merely roses with long scrambling shoots which can be trained up fences and walls. Most of them prefer the sunny side of a fence, though some will thrive in the shade.

Training bushes against fences
Apart from the true climbing plants, one should also remember

that most bushes with long branches can be trained against fences and walls. These include *Forsythia suspensa* 'Sieboldii', many cotoneasters, ceanothus and some viburnums.

Trained shrubs and climbing plants have the unfortunate feature of becoming bare and ugly at the base, so it is advisable to have some low ground cover along the foot of the fence.

17   Early Spring along the Drive

A carport or garage is often situated well back on a plot, but by locating it just 4–5m (about 15ft) closer, one could make use of its walls as a background for an attractive sitting-out area. It is wise to separate any drive-way from the garden with a broad grouping of plants, which should preferably be equally attractive on both sides. This creates a welcoming sort of garden. In Plate 17 this has been done with a belt of spring-flowering shrubs and a single yew.

The ground between the shrubs is covered with both spring flowering and evergreen ground-cover plants, which (as always recommended) are planted in large areas of up to several square metres.

The number of ground-cover plants required can be quite surprising and can often cost more than the shrubs themselves; but it pays not to skimp. Ground-cover plants should always be bought by the box as nurseries often give a bulk order rebate.

The patient gardener can save a great deal of money by cultivating a number of the best ground-cover plants himself. A small piece of stem and a little root separated from a bigger plot develops very quickly.

Separation by hedge or fence

One can also separate the drive from the garden with a trimmed or free-growing hedge or a wooden fence. The latter is an excellent solution for the impatient gardener. Neither the hedge nor the fence should be placed right up to the drive, or it will give it the appearance of a narrow gorge. Both hedges and fences should be placed a couple of yards in, so that room is left for a broad border along the drive. In this one could plant primarily ground-cover plants, for example lesser periwinkle, with groups of bulbs and with some shrubs and smaller trees here and there. Alternatively one could underplant with the somewhat taller *Cotoneaster hybridus* 'Skogholm'.

18   Planting along Low Walls

The walls shown on this plate could either be low structures retaining a terrace behind, where a slope has been levelled, or one side of a rockery which consists of two retaining walls with earth between, and is planted in the same way as a one-sided wall. Such rockery walls can give shelter and also separate the terrace from the garden in a less abrupt way than a fence would. One can sit undisturbed behind a rockery wall and yet be in contact with the garden behind.

A rockery wall must be about 1m (3ft) wide otherwise there is neither the volume of earth nor enough room to ensure adequate dampness and a proper arrangement of plants. At the same time they provide the good drainage which many alpines prefer rather than the ill-drained or compacted soil on the level.

Retaining walls
Retaining walls can be built of various materials, but only one type should be used in the same garden. There are many kinds of precast walling blocks, natural stone slabs, or large boulders can be used. The soil behind a retaining wall can expand in heavy frost and push the stones outwards, and the same may occur in very wet weather. Such calamities can be forestalled by placing a thick layer of gravel under and behind the wall. A retaining wall of 60–80cm (2–2½ft) will be stable if gravel is laid to a depth of 40cm (about 1½ft) giving a slope backwards of about 15% of the height of the wall, the bottom course stones being placed below ground level. The gravel should be brought up behind the wall to two-thirds of its height. Flat slabs should be staggered to create the slope or 'batter' necessary at the front, but they should not slope backwards to any degree.

Wall plants should be placed in the wall during building, as it is almost impossible to get them to root successfully at a later stage. With regular slabs it may be necessary to break off about 2cm (1in) from one end to leave room for a plant. On no account must one leave more room between the slabs or the bonding will be irregular. The plant should be arranged so that only a little of it protrudes from the hole. Place earth around the roots, which have been well spread out, to create as large a surface area as possible. The danger is lack of moisture. If the roots do not have complete contact with the damp earth behind the wall, the plant will die quickly. Contact is improved if the plant is watered on planting and when the wall is finished.

Plants should not be set in too low down as many of them form large cushions which should be allowed to hang freely.

Slabs can be used to top the wall but it is often more attractive to plant here too. The same plants can be used as in the sides, but if one prefers a slightly higher arrangement, then small shrubs such as berberis, potentilla and pyracantha can be planted. One could also imagine a low arrangement of *Cotoneaster hybridus* 'Pendulus', *Stephenandra incisa*, or spreading junipers. A third possibility is to plant groups of perennials, particularly those which will tolerate dryness, such as *Coreopsis verticillata* 'Grandiflora', *Salvia superba* 'East Friesland' and *Sedum spectabile*.

19 Plants for a North-facing Wall

In the northern hemisphere, the north side of a house or fence is an excellent position for most evergreen, leaf-bearing trees and shrubs, which often prefer to be out of direct sun. However, poor growth conditions are often found against house walls. The flowerbed is often narrow and situated under broad eaves, so that it is sheltered from rain. What is more, the soil often consists mainly of rubble from building. Beds should therefore be re-made by digging down to a depth of 50cm and filling with good, porous topsoil. Ideally beds should be 1m (3ft) or more wide. In Plate 19, the border is about 3m (10ft) wide and this is not too much, for it is not only a question of soil, but also that of having sufficient room for the plants that matters. In broader borders, one can plant larger shrubs and smaller trees, thus increasing the assortment of plants to choose from. Plant also as much ground-cover as possible, as recommended in the Introduction.

Even when beds by walls have been re-made, plenty of water will be essential in hot dry weather.

20   Plants for a South-facing Wall

It is always a good principle to plant generously and closely around the house and terrace. A house should appear to grow out of the vegetation; plants bring the cold wall surfaces and large glazed areas to life, while from within the rooms it is delightful to be able to look out on to a mass of lush plants.

As with the north-facing border, provide as much width as possible. The border in Plate 20 is about 2m (6½ft) wide. One must remember to take the habit of growth of plants into consideration when planning the beds. The area immediately under the eaves is a poor position for growth, although bulbs like nerines which need summer baking will thrive there. In any case the need for water is even greater on account of the faster evaporation near the warm, dry, south-facing wall.

However, it is a good idea to lay a row of paving stones close by the wall, as it is an asset for the window cleaner and helps to retain moisture in the driest part of the garden. A row of paving stones 25–50cm (10–12in) wide would not be noticed once there is a wide bed of lush plants in front of it which would spread over the edges of the stones.

A choice of plants

In the northern hemisphere, many tender plants which would prove quite hopeless less further out in the garden will thrive by a south-facing wall. Here one can try planting exotics like *Albizzia julibrissin*, *Clianthus puniceus* and *Fremontodendron californicum*.

However, climbing roses seldom do well on a hot, south-facing wall. They suffer from red spider mite, which causes the leaves to turn bronze and eventually fall off, and mildew, a fungus encouraged by warmth and dryness. Regular spraying against these troubles will help.

Clematis also need special care if placed up against south-facing walls. They need to have moisture and some shade at the roots, which must be surrounded with peaty soil and plants for shade. Higher up, clematis will appreciate the warmth of the wall which will then encourage regular flowering.

Unusual evergreen ground cover
A south-facing border can be planted out in many ways. A good mixture of plants is suggested in Plate 20. Another type of arrangement can be made by covering the whole area with *Iberis sempervirens* 'Little Gem', a perennial candytuft which produces a mass of white flowers in the spring. Within this can be planted groups of tall tulips and various lilies which will bloom at a later time, with perhaps a few summer hyacinths, *Galtonia candicans*; a couple of late-flowering *Amaryllis belladonna*, belladonna lilies, would also look good. A single corkscrew hazel, *Corylus avellana* 'Contorta', a *Caryopteris clandonensis* and a *Viburnum burkwoodii* might also be planted among the ground cover, with possibly a rose here and there. To complete the picture, a big square of ice plant, *Sedum spectabile* 'Brilliant' and possibly a *Salvia superba* 'East Friesland', might be added.

21 Conifers

Plate 21 shows an attractive corner of the garden with an arrangement which could equally well have been used elsewhere. One can imagine that it would be pleasant to sit on the terrace and look out over such pleasant and characteristic ground cover. Alternatively, one could arrange the group just outside the living room window, as many modern windows reach from floor to ceiling and really need an interesting garden outside. The whole arrangement only takes 30 sq. m (about 320 sq. ft).

Ground cover
The ground cover shown in the foreground is a handsome and long-flowering carpet of heather, *Erica carnea*, which is very easy to establish in ordinary garden soil. The many available varieties of this heather flower over many months and are not lime-hating like *Calluna vulgaris*, the ling. A group of blue fescue, *Festuca ovina* 'Glauca', limits the heather ground cover.

Evergreen backgrounds for colourful flowers
Groups of narcissi have been planted among all the greenery, but tulips could also have been used provided that their colours blended with the rhododendrons in the background. For later

blooming one could use lilies, the gladiolus relation *Acidanthera bicolor* and the summer hyacinth *Galtonia candicans*. There is a vast number of lilies available so that one is able to choose varieties to ensure blossom through summer to autumn; also lily-of-the-valley and *Polygonatum multiflorum*, Solomon's seal, are most effective in May and June.

22 Evergreen Trees and Shrubs

To conceal walls, fences, sheds or other unsightly constructions, a group of leaf-bearing evergreens is advisable, such as those suggested in Plate 22.

Unlike conifers, many leaf-bearing evergreens have colourful blossom, whilst others have fruits which liven up the late autumn months which really need colour. This is true of *Cotoneaster salicifolius floccosus*, *Ilex aquifolium* (holly) varieties, *Pernettya mucronata*, *Pyracantha coccinea* and *Skimmia japonica*.

Renewal by pruning
Leaf-bearing evergreens tolerate pruning, some of them even heavy pruning. One can shape them as one chooses, even to the extent of the topiary work often seen on box to produce animals and other shapes. Many, such as *Berberis verruculosa*, box, holly and pyracantha are suitable for trimmed hedges. Even free-growing bushes need to be pruned now and then to prevent them becoming too tall and straggly. For example, this is true of *Mahonia aquifolium*, which shoots well even if it has been pruned back almost to ground level, and *Prunus laurocerasus* the cherry laurel.

23–24 Bright Flowerbeds for Spring

Flowering bulbs, springtime and colour all belong together. In Europe and North America, the grey winter needs a festive finale early in the New Year. Thus a good imagination is needed to plant the right bulbs in the right places. One can often take note of some good varieties seen in parks and gardens, but to get from these ideas to a good result in one's own garden is nevertheless quite a job. The effect must not be garish and the mass effect used in parks is normally quite unsuitable in the average garden.

Bulbs – a special way of life

Bulbs can develop both leaves and flowers with no other outside addition than water. It is not even necessary to have a great deal of light, as long as there is enough for the leaves to turn green. For this reason bulbs can be planted anywhere and they will grow happily. But if they are to bloom again in following years, they should have rich soil and plenty of light. Most of the small spring bulbs like scillas, muscari and crocuses will continue to flower for years. Daffodils will do so in open situations, but tulips do so less readily – except for the 'botanical' varieties, which often survive and flower for many years.

Early spring bulbs such as aconites, crocuses, grape hyacinths, scillas and snowdrops develop very quickly. They develop new bulbs, capable of flowering, within a couple of months. Therefore, they survive fairly well under deciduous trees and bushes because they have finished growing well before the trees and bushes have begun to provide much shade. Narcissi and tulips take much longer to develop and must be planted so that they have a chance to grow. For the same reason, these bulbs cannot be planted in the lawn as the grass would have grown extremely high before the bulbs were mature – though they can be planted in rough grassy areas. However, small early bulbs can be planted in a lawn as they will have finished developing before the grass-cutting season begins. The lawn can be cut as usual, whilst the bulbs lie buried, waiting for next spring.

As can be seen from the above information, one should never cut off the green leaves of tulips or other bulbs as soon as they have flowered. This will surely prevent the bulbs blooming again next spring; indeed it is likely to finish them off! To see bulbs die down is part of the garden picture. Many gardeners cut off the seed pods of narcissi and tulips once they have flowered so that all nourishment goes to the bulb; the formation of seeds can certainly weaken the next year's bulb. One can, however, allow small bulbs to keep their seeds; they are not weakened as much by going to seed and new bulbs grow very rapidly – so that whole carpets are formed in a few years. One should never dig between bushes where these small bulbs have been planted or the small seedlings may easily be damaged.

Colour arrangements

One should work consciously with colours in order to choose the correct plan for bulb flowers. Pastel shades of pink, lilac, white and cream tulips certainly go well together, but the whole effect would be spoiled if a group of bright red tulips was planted in the middle. If one wishes to work with red, this should only be mixed with yellow and orange, avoiding other colours. The early, low red varieties of tulip like 'Fusilier' and 'Princeps' look attractive with yellow daffodils, and the late, tall, red Darwin tulips look splendid with blue Siberian Bugloss, *Brunnera macrophylla*.

Contrasts can also be attractive; white lily-flowered tulips have a graceful aspect when underplanted with blue forget-me-not; whole grape hyacinths, which have a very long flowering period, look wonderful in large groups between red tulips. The fine botanical tulips should not be forgotten. Groups of 8–10 bulbs between rhododendrons are quite lovely. One should also remember to include *Fritillaria imperialis*, crown imperial, in the same company. It has red and yellow forms and does not seem to mind a little shade.

Using bulbs and tubers

Most bulbs look their prettiest when used among other plants. Tall, late-flowering tulips can be planted among early-flowering perennials and roses, and the very early-flowering botanical tulips, crocuses and scillas in the rockery. Among evergreen shrubs, narcissi and lily-flowering tulips look best when planted in groups, keeping each variety separate. Small bulbs such as aconites, crocuses and snowdrops can be planted in the lawn, near a shrub, or along the drive, but they are at their prettiest when peeping through green ground cover plants such as *Cotoneaster dammeri* and *Vinca minor*.

Flowerbeds devoted to bulbs underplanted with other spring flowers can be most appealing in the lawn near the terrace, as can be seen in Plates 23–24. This use of bulbs is expensive though, as everything is taken up after flowering and new bulbs are planted in the autumn. Formal beds of spring bulbs can be square, rectangular or circular, but regardless of the shape, they should not be less than 1 sq. m (11 sq. ft), preferably 2–3 sq. m (about 25 sq. ft).

25–26 Beautiful Herbaceous Borders

Many gardeners have an aversion to herbaceous borders. Too much is made of the amount of work allegedly entailed in weeding, division and cutting back after flowering. It was the herbaceous borders of a generation ago which were so off-putting and that is a pity, for we cannot do without perennials. In fact, perennials can look after themselves, almost like a close arrangement of shrubs. It simply depends on choosing the right varieties and types and planting them so that they mingle naturally with the other plants in the garden. Perennials can be planted among shrubs or they can be assembled in beds on their own. The majority of arrangements and plans in this book include perennials, but not one herbaceous border has been planted in the old-fashioned manner.

Where and how to plant
If the herbaceous plant area adjoins a hedge, it is wise to have a flagged path alongside, for the roots of hedges extend a long way. A young privet hedge has superficial roots which extend for some way on either side. A strip of paving creates good growth conditions for both the hedge and the perennials since roots like to run about in the dampness under paving stones. At the same time, it eases the task of hedge-cutting and allows one to enjoy the herbaceous border from both sides.

A herbaceous border containing different plants and varieties, but only a few of each type, has no character. It is wiser to use several plants of each variety together with at least three, and possibly up to a dozen, together – the result is well worth it. It is also a good idea to buy a box of each perennial instead of just a few; it often works out cheaper.

In the old days it was usual to plant the shortest perennials in the foreground and the tallest at the back. It was regarded as a virtue to plant perennials so that they graduated in height in a regimented way. A herbaceous border planted like that is dull: today one often plants low perennials among the taller ones in large expanses.

Four herbaceous borders
Four examples of beautiful herbaceous borders are shown in

Plates 25–26. Plots of this type should not be less than 2 sq. m (21 sq. ft) in area and look best with 3 to 5 plots placed together in a sunny lawn. When planting, surround tall decorative perennials with shorter ones and ensure that the bed can be in flower throughout the summer.

Perennials with evergreens
Perennials can create variety when planted among evergreen bushes. Suitable for this purpose are *Adonis amurensis*, *Anemone hybrida* 'Queen Charlotte' (a Japanese anemone), *Bergenia cordifolia* 'Purpurea', *Brunnera macrophylla*, *Cimicifuga racemosa*, *Epimedium rubrum*, *Helleborus niger* and *H.orientalis*, (Christmas and Lenten roses), *Heuchera sanguinea* 'Pluie de Feu', *Polygonatum multiflorum*, *Rodgersia pinnata*, *Thalictrum dipterocarpum* and *Veronica longifolia*, all of which will tolerate some shade and most of which have attractive leaves.

Never dig between perennials as it disturbs the fine roots and prevents the small bulbs such as aconite, crocus, grape hyacinth, scilla and snowdrop from spreading freely by seeding. Far rather introduce a layer of leaf mould or weed-free compost in between the plants to retain the moisture, prevent frost from penetrating and improve the soil to the advantage of the vegetation. Fertilizer should be sprinkled evenly between the plants, which can die if the fertilizer is placed too close to the neck of the root. It can also badly scorch the leaves if any granules should lodge on them. There is no other way of broadcasting fertilizer than by hand. Apply a balanced fertilizer such as National 'Growmore' in the early spring at the recommended rate, and the same quantity again later on in the early summer, and fork it in lightly.

Many perennials become dry in an upright position when they fade in the autumn. When hard frost or snow settles on these dead flowerheads, they develop a beauty which is almost as striking as their summer flowers. The dry tops also protect the new shoots in the spring, so let them remain in place throughout the winter.

27 Flowerbeds for Late Summer

Spring's gay beds can be replaced by late summer beds which are just as colourful (in Plate 27). The plants used in these beds are long-flowering annuals, bulbs and tubers which have been planted in spring.

The colours in the bed on the left are bright and kept in the 'warm' shades. The bed on the right shows the effective use of pastel shades. A bed of this type looks at its best when set back in the garden.

Long-flowering annuals
Provided that they are given sufficient water and nourishment, the majority of annuals have a long flowering period, right up until the first night frost kills them in late summer or early autumn. Take care when applying nitrogenous fertilizers as several annuals (among others the tropaeolum family) produce no flowers and only develop a mass of leaves if they receive too much. Also, it is important to dead-head, not only for the sake of appearance, but also to prevent seed development which causes the plant to stop forming buds. If these rules are obeyed, then plants such as the low blue ageratum, the white marguerite (*Chrysanthemum frutescens*) and the yellow annual chrysanthemum 'Eastern Star' will bloom until the frost catches them; the tall and short varieties of tagetes will continue blooming in bright yellow and orange even after the first night frost.

Late-flowering bulbs and tubers
Acidanthera bicolor, tigridia or tiger flower, gladioli, *Hyacinthus candicans* the summer hyacinth, ixia the African corn lily, *Montbretia crocosmiiflora* and several other fleshy rooted plants are not completely hardy in this country, particularly in colder latitudes, so they should be planted out in the spring having been over-wintered in a frostfree place. Lilies are also bulbs but can remain in the ground during winter. Most of the plants just mentioned do not flower until late summer or autumn.

The positioning of these plants is never any trouble, as they can be planted singly or in groups where there is room. The tall, graceful *Montbretia crocosmiiflora* would look most attractive among closely planted low ageratum in one of the garden's autumn beds. Dahlias and gladioli include many very bright colours so care should be taken when arranging them; however, if they are dead-headed daily, they will bloom for a long time.

Both are particularly successful as cut flowers, and for that very reason it is a good idea to have a couple of rows of them in the garden. Never plant dahlias to fill out gaps between small, newly planted bushes or these will have to pay the penalty of being inconspicuous by having to stand in the shadow of these 'young cuckoos'.

Beds for late summer
To make the herbaceous border even more beautiful and colourful in late summer, one should plant some long flowering, late-blooming bulbs and tubers as mentioned earlier. However, do remember to choose plants whose habit of growth does not seem out of place amongst other perennials. Annuals are also suitable for this purpose and apart from the numerous tagetes and zinnia varieties, ought to include *Chrysanthemum frutescens*, tobacco plant, *Rudbeckia hirta* or Gloriosa daisies, annual scabious and *Verbena venosa*. Plants in a rockery can be supplemented in the same way by using annuals, provided they are not over-improved varieties or hybrids. Unobtrusive plants such as *Alyssum maritimum* 'Little Dorrit' and 'Violet Queen', *Iberis umbellata* the annual candytuft, *Lobelia* 'Hamburgia', *Portulaca grandiflora*, and *Sanvitalia procumbens* the 'creeping zinnia' would be suitable. It would be most inadvisable to plant hybrid plants such as begonias, geraniums, large flowered dahlias and double stocks among the low cushions of rock plants whose habits of growth have often been influenced by their natural surroundings.

28–30   Roses in Good Company

Despite their great beauty, roses can be some of the most difficult plants to arrange attractively and harmoniously in the garden. There are two reasons for this; firstly the habit of growth is not particularly pretty and secondly during the winter months the plant hardly covers the surface of the bed in which it is planted. Roses have what one calls 'ugly legs'. The old-fashioned idea of planting roses in parallel lines with large gaps between each tends to expose the 'legs' even more, because the ground between the plants is never covered. Today, the aim should be to have not one single square inch of bare soil. Rose purists may object to anything growing among their plants, but in non-specialised gardens other plants can certainly enhance the roses.

The varieties of rose include an enormous number of colours with every possible shade of red, pink, yellow, and white that one could imagine.* Many of these colours blend harmoniously together, but one can find shades, especially among reds, which can clash abominably. For example, a clear pink floribunda rose such as 'Polka' ruins the clear red variety 'Sarabande'. Generally speaking, one can say that bright clear, red roses – not bluish–red shades – can be planted with orange and clear yellow varieties, whilst pink roses in various shades should only be arranged with white varieties.

Blue, white and mauve backgrounds

If one follows the guide-lines with regard to colours, then one should have beautiful rose beds. A most striking effect would be produced by planting some annuals or perennials with blue, white, mauve and in some casess yellow flowers to keep the roses company. A peaceful dark background of evergreen trees and shrubs would help to emphasise the full beauty of the roses.

Whatever happens do not choose varieties of bright red flowers as it is over reds that the greatest difficulties occur: plants such as many begonias, geraniums and salvias would be disastrous if planted amongst roses. This also applies to perennials such as scarlet luchnis and the bright red varieties of phlox. Allow a year for the roses to become established before planting the companion plants.

Annuals for small rose beds

In small rose beds of $1\frac{1}{4} \times 1\frac{1}{4}$m (12–13 sq. ft) or so, low annuals (and possibly a few rock plants along the outer edge of the bed) should be used for preference. The rock plants will prettily soften the edge of any path which frames the rose beds. The latter applies to larger rose beds too.

The following annuals can be recommended: *Ageratum* 'Imperial Dwarf', *Felicia amelloides*, blue lobelias, and *Verbena*

---

*See also Edland, H., *The Pocket Encyclopaedia of Roses in Colour* Blandford Press Ltd.

venosa; all of which bear blue-toned flowers which complemen
roses of any colour. The low, carpet-forming *Alyssum maritimun*
'Little Dorrit' and 'Violet Queen', white and violet, have a lovely
scent and can be sown directly between the rose bushes. Yellow
flowering annuals such as tagetes in the varieties 'Harmony'
'Marietta', 'Rusty Red' and 'Sunbeam' make good colour con
trasts to orange–red and clear red roses.

The following rock plants can be recommended for planting
along the outside edge of the rose beds: *Aubrieta* 'Crimson King'
'Dr. Mules' and 'Lavender', *Campanula portenschlagiana, Cerastium
biebersteinii*, garden pinks (dianthus) like 'Duchess of Fife' and
Thymus serpyllum 'Splendens'. All these have bluish–mauve, pale
pink or white flowers.

Perennials for larger rose beds
In rose beds of more than 3 sq. m (32 sq. ft), where roses are
planted in groups of 3–7 with about 30–40cm (8–12in) between
the groups, one can use larger and more vigorous plants, especi
ally perennials. The pretty, scented lavender makes a framing
edge provided the bed is large enough for the roses not to be
swamped. The following perennials, which all have blue or
bluish–mauve flowers, can also be recommended: *Aster amellus*
'Blue King', 'King George' and 'Mauve Queen', the lower
growing varieties of delphinium, and *Salvia superba* 'East Friesland'. Perennials with white or pale pink flowers such as *Achillea
sibirica, Astrantia major*, and *Gypsophila paniculata* 'Bristol Fairy' are
also suitable.

For the outer edge of the beds, the following low perennials can
be planted: *Aubrieta* 'Crimson King', 'Dr. Mules' and 'Lavender',
Dianthus 'Duchess of Fife' and other pinks, *Stachys lanata*, lamb's
ears, and *Veronica incana*. All have bluish–mauve, pale pink or
white flowers and the last three plants have beautiful grey leaves
which would also complement white and pink roses.

Evergreen backgrounds
Dark red or bright yellow roses should never be planted against
red or yellow brick walls. To display such roses to advantage,
they should be planted against a background of dark evergreen
trees and shrubs as illustrated in Plate 30. The effect is one of

hiding the roses' ugly 'feet and legs' with a peaceful, fresh green ground-cover of low or creeping evergreens. Under these conditions the roses should be planted in groups of 5–9 bushes, leaving about 30–50cm (1–1½ft) between the groups, according to the different varieties' habits of growth. Each group consists of several plants of the same variety of rose, which are not pruned too heavily and are thus able to grow together; this gives the appearance of one large bush. Some vigorous varieties suitable for such a bed are as follows: 'Chinatown', 'Fragrant Cloud', 'Hanne', 'Korona', 'Evelyn Fison', 'Peace', 'Queen Elizabeth', 'Sutter's Gold', 'Uncle Walter', and 'Whisky Mac'.

Preferably, the background bushes should have shiny, dark green leaves, e.g. holly, *Ilex aquifolium*, which is well suited because its prickly leaves have a certain visual similarity to those of roses. The large-leafed box, *Buxus sempervirens* 'Bullata', the Oregon grape, *Mahonia aquifolium*, and the cherry laurel, *Prunus laurocerasus* 'Otto Luyken', would be also excellent as a background, as would indeed the dark green yew, *Taxus baccata*.

The following low, evergreen ground cover plants can be recommended: *Asarum europaeum*, *Cotoneaster dammeri* and *Vinca minor*, among which scilla and other spring bulbs can be planted. Among tall roses, a few mahonias could be planted as they are of moderate growth and can be cut back each spring. Finally, some groups of white Regal lilies, *Lilium regale*, would look lovely among the roses.

31 A Garden for Cut Flowers

Many annuals are so vivid that they are difficult to arrange among other plants in the garden. Apart from that, they leave a gap from the first night frost until early the next summer. If flowers for the house are in much demand it is a sensible idea to have a garden especially for flowers for cutting. Such a garden should be at least 5 metres wide and placed far enough away from any hedges or trees with aggressive roots to allow natural growth and plenty of light, preferably full sun.

Dividing the garden by paths
If the flower garden is divided by flagged paths, it makes cul-

tivating and cutting the flowers much easier. In beds a good 1m (3ft) wide, this allows one to reach to the middle from either side of the path. The flagged path also improves the conditions for growth, because the plant roots can creep under the flagstones in order to reach the damp soil there. The soil may be improved in spring by the addition of peat, and artificial fertilizer should also be given – and as for the rest of the garden one should be careful of the amount of nitrogen, because many annuals 'forget' to flower and will produce only leaves if fed too much nitrogen.

Annuals for cutting
Hardy annuals are most suitable as they can be sown directly in the beds from late March onwards when the weather promises a warm spell after sowing; thus the seeds do not rot in the soil.

When the small plants are well established, showing three or four true leaves, they should be thinned out according to the variety. For example zinnias should be grown with 10cm (4in) between each plant. It is often difficult for the amateur to realize at first just how much room each plant will take eventually. but this thinning – to the distance recommended on the seed packet – is absolutely essential if plants are not to grow spindly and flower prematurely.

Most hardy annuals are suitable for cutting for the house and the following varieties last specially well when picked: calendulas or pot marigolds, *Callistephus chinensis* or China asters, *Centaurea cyanus* the cornflower, *Cosmos bipinnatus*, larkspurs, clarkia, *Nigella damascena* or Love-in-the-mist, annual scabious and *Verbena venosa* (really a perennial but can be treated as an annual). Ornamental grasses such as *Lagurus ovatus* and *Briza major* can be added.

Many annuals will overwinter in well-drained soil if sown in early September; they will then flower early the following summer.

Roses and perennials for cutting
Flowers for cutting should certainly include others beside annuals. There are numerous perennials which will last well in vases. If one does not like roses in ornamental gardens, they can be planted in the plot for cut flowers, but choose varieties carefully as not all roses are suitable for vases. Most hybrid teas are excellent and

also the floribundas with h.t.-type blooms. Grow a good colour range.

Perennials for cutting can be planted in rows with 2–3 blocks of each variety, in the same way as annuals. Flowers in rows can be quite as beautiful as the rest of the garden. The following perennials are recommended for cutting: *Achillea filipendulina* 'Parker's Variety', *Aster amellus* varieties, *Chrysanthemum coccineum* 'E. M. Robinson', *Coreopsis verticillata* 'Grandiflora', *Erigeron* varieties, *Gypsophila paniculata* 'Bristol Fairy', *Helenium hybridum* 'Moerheim Beauty', *Heliopsis scabra* 'Patula', *Liatris spicata*, and *Lysimachia clethroides*. The last, white loosestrife, lasts particularly well in water and looks splendid with roses, as does *Astrantia major*, the masterwort, which in spite of its modest appearance is the best perennial to lighten a heavy bouquet of red roses.

Bulbs and tubers
Among bulbs and tubers, later-flowering tulips, dahlias and gladioli are specially recommended. Tulips that keep well in water include 'Copeland's Favourite', 'Demeter', 'Golden Harvest', 'Gudoshnik', 'Mamassa', 'Queen of Bartigons' and 'Queen of Sheba'. Remember to leave behind a couple of leaves when cutting, to ensure that the bulbs flower next year, even though the flowers will be smaller.

Among dahlias, try 'Best Seller', 'Brandaris', 'La Cierva', 'Gerrie Hoek', 'Goldelse', 'Good Morning', 'Hugin', 'Komet', 'Oslo', 'Purple King', 'Requiem', 'Sonja' and 'White Favourite'. Few dahlias do not last well when cut.

Recommended gladioli include 'Blue Conqueror', 'Flowersong', 'Life Flame', 'Perosi' and 'Peter Pears'. Gladiolus corms and dahlia tubers are planted in spring and taken up in autumn when the night frosts have killed the top, and stored in a dry, frost-free place.

32 A Green Garden

An enclosed area of about 75 sq. m (800 sq. ft) placed in the middle of a large garden, or at its far end, can provide an intriguing atmosphere if, as shown in Plate 32, it has been planted with trees growing freely in a carpet of spring bulbs and woodland plants with narrow winding paths between. At the same time, it will be an easy area to maintain. If one chooses short trees, the green garden can remain unchanged for many years. The following trees of moderate growth are to be recommended: *Acer ginnala*, *A.rufinerve*, *Amelanchier canadensis*, *Cercidiphyllum japonicum* and *Rhus typhina*. All of them are beautiful as the leaves unfold, have attractive foliage and intense colours in the autumn. Larger trees such as *Metasequoia glyptostroboides* the dawn redwood, *Ailanthus altissima* the tree of heaven, and possibly birches might also be considered. In Plate 23, the following trees are illustrated: *Acer platanoides*, Norway Maple, *Liriodendron tulipifera*, tulip tree, *Pterocarya fraxinifolia*, wing nut, and *Quercus borealis*, red oak. The crowns of these have been pruned to form a roof of leaves. The larger trees must be kept in check by cutting back, or one must plant a new tree each year; then after about ten years one can begin to cut down some of the largest. In that way the green garden can be kept young for ever.

Woodland spring bulbs and ferns

Throughout the woodland, larger and smaller groups of spring bulbs should be planted: aconites, crocuses, grape hyacinths, scillas, snowdrops, crown imperials, erythroniums, narcissi and 'botanical' tulips. Gradually these will seed themselves and spread so that eventually the natural balance is found. Several ferns, *Dicentra spectabilis* the bleeding heart, and *Polygonatum multiflorum*, Solomon's seal, can be planted as ground cover together with *Corydalis lutea*, yellow fumitory, *Vinca minor*, lesser periwinkle, *Waldsteinia ternata* and *Hedera helix*, ivy – which can climb up the trees too: there are many variegated forms.

The winding paths should not be covered with paving stones or other hard substances, but should either remain as earth paths, possibly strewn with some gravel, or they could be covered with a 4–5cms thick layer of pine needles. Pine needles form an attractive, soft carpet which blends well with the surroundings and has the advantage of keeping one's feet dry. The only maintenance that the pine-needle path needs is an extra layer once a year!

33   A 'Wild' Garden

To create artificially 'true nature' as it is found in a meadow is the most difficult part of the art of gardening. Nature's planning and planting are the results of mutual competition, soil, humidity, light and temperature. The chance flora which evolves is difficult to imitate in a garden.

However, even with a little artistic sense, one can come a long way. Do not dig or use other coarse tools, and weed only by hand or with a weeding fork in order to avoid damage to the young seedlings. One must learn to recognize these seedlings and they can then be thinned out or perhaps moved and the plants allowed to seed themselves. It is difficult to plant 'naturally' and one has to remember to go along with nature's balance. There are gardeners who plant narcissus bulbs by throwing a bag of them up in the air and planting them just where they fall. In this way the most casual and natural-looking grouping can be created. The meadow of flowers shown in Plate 33 is based on groups of ground-covering perennials, bulbs and tubers naturally arranged between graceful trees and bushes.

A lawn of wild flowers
A variation of a meadow of flowers is a lawn of wild flowers in a carpet of grass with all types of bulbs and tubers, wild flowers of the field, perennials, trees and bushes.

Seeing how easily weeds run amok in a garden, one would have thought that it was an easy task to create a lawn of flowers. Is it just a case of letting everything grow wild? Unfortunately, no. A lawn of flowers is the equivalent of a wayside verge and therefore not a truly natural product. It can only exist if the grass is cut now and then or has animals grazing on it. Daisies, which create one of the finest lawns of flowers one could imagine, can only exist if the lawn is cut occasionally and the grass is weak and undernourished.

Nature's nourishment cycle
A lawn of flowers must not be fed. It will thrive on poor, 'starved' soil. Preferably there should be trees and large shrubs in the grass to create root competition which will hamper the growth of the grass. The lawn should be sown with a weak-growing variety, for

example fiorin grass (*Agrostis alba*). One should sow less liberally than for a traditional lawn, using about ½ kg of seed per 100 sq. m (1 lb per 120 sq. yds).

Perennials in groups
Many perennials would thrive in a lawn of flowers, for example columbine, gypsophila, globeflower, knapweed, lupin, marguerite and poppy, all of which can be planted after the grass has appeared. Place planks of wood, flower pots or buckets on the ground when sowing the grass seed, then there will be clear patches in which to plant the perennials. After flowering, the lawn should be cut with a scythe, after which some of the perennials will flower again; alternatively one can plant large areas and mow the grass between them. It will not matter if some tall grass remains at the edge of the perennials; that is a part of any lawn of flowers.

The early bulbs and tubers grown, such as aconite, crocus, scilla and snowdrop, should be allowed to remain undisturbed until the leaves wither – around the first week in June – when one can cut the grass in order to achieve a new green. These spring flowers will have had time to form new bulbs and tubers before they die down completely. Narcissi and tulips present more of a problem as they require a longer time to mature. It is wise to plant them in groups, so that one can mow around them until the leaves die down – otherwise the grass grows too high.

34   A Lily Garden

Every garden is improved by subdivision and a small lily garden of about 50 sq. m (60 sq. yds), such as that illustrated in Plate 34, could be placed in any garden of about 600–800 sq. m (700–1000 sq. yds). The fence which forms the boundary of the lily garden gives the graceful lilies their own frame and does not need to be closely woven. It is possible to have all manner of plants climbing up such a fence, where they would enjoy a quite different and more natural habitat than up against a warm, south-facing wall, where many of these damp-loving woodland plants have to endure life.

Beauty throughout the summer
Like all bulbs, lilies should be planted in larger or smaller groups

amongst low ground vegetation. This should consist of, for example, *Cotoneaster dammeri* or *Vinca minor*, with graceful and not too colourful neighbours as shown in the Plate 24. Apart from the lilies, a number of other plants are also included. If early-flowering bulbs are planted among ground-cover plants, you can enjoy flowers right through to the end of summer, when the last lilies flower.

The plant collector's paradise
The lily garden is decidedly a 'collector's piece', but for once it is aesthetic too. Beauty and a mania for collecting can be combined splendidly. The idea can be extended to include outdoor orchids among the ground-cover plants and perhaps a few deciduous rhododendrons – but then one must remember to plant them in pockets of acid soil. The lily garden is an idea capable of development according to conditions. Whether it be square, octagonal, 12-sided, or round is immaterial, as long as it is a beautiful space with beautiful plants.

Cultivation of lilies
During the last few years a number of new hybrids of lily have been developed which are often more beautiful than the old varieties – and also much easier to grow.

Lilies have bulbs just like narcissi and tulips, but differ from them in that they do not have any real resting period without roots. Therefore the bulbs should be treated carefully when they are out of the earth. They must not be allowed to dry out or become warm. Ideally, lily bulbs should be planted in autumn, but they are usually not available to the gardener until spring.

Continuous dampness must be avoided if lilies are to be grown; avoid areas with compacted clay and waterlogged subsoil. On such soils they can be grown in raised beds prepared by loosening the subsoil and placing 15–20cm (6–8ins) of light soil on top. A low stone wall is also an excellent situation, because lilies do well in very porous soil. To produce this one can blend an equal part mixture of ordinary garden soil, sand and peat. Most lily bulbs should be planted quite deeply, as the roots are formed from the section of stem immediately above the bulb.

One must not expect lilies to develop their full beauty the first year, as it takes a while before they can achieve this. If they like the position they will spread and form beautiful groups.

Lillies as cut flowers
Lilies last successfully in water, but one must remember that it is the stem and leaves which provide nourishment for the new flowering bulbs. It is wise, therefore, to cut the flowers with as short a stem as possible and to limit cutting to just a few plants in each group. Remember not to cut down the stems after flowering, because lilies, like other bulbs, need to die down naturally; new bulbs can then secure maximum nourishment for development. The seed pods of lilies are large and elegant and definitely contribute to the general impression of the plant.

Modern varieties of lily
Throughout the last 30 years lilies have been improved constantly to produce new hybrids. Here is a selection of the best:

Upward-facing lilies: 'Enchantment', orange–red, 'Croesus', clear yellow, 'Cinnabar', dark red, 'Burgundy', wine red, 'Destiny', lemon yellow, 'Golden Charlie', golden yellow, 'Joan Evans', sulphur yellow, 'Prosperity', pale yellow, and 'Harmony', orange–yellow.

Turk's-cap lilies: 'Amber Gold', butter yellow, 'Citronella', lemon yellow, 'Corsage', ivory coloured with brown spots in the throat, 'Discovery', dark wine red, 'Harlequin Hybrids' (a mixture) and 'Sonata', orange.

Trumpet lilies: 'Black Dragon', white and yellow with dark brown outside, 'Green Magic', white with darker outside, 'Golden Splendour', yellow with reddish outside, 'Pink Perfection', shaded red, 'Olympic Hybrid', white, 'Royal Gold', golden yellow.

Oriental hybrids (really sumptuous – but rather expensive): 'Empress of India', 150cms tall with 25cm flowers of dark red; 'Imperial Silver' and 'Imperial Gold' which have white flowers with silver and gold tinges, respectively.

Finally, a practical tip. If one is not a specialist, one should buy the cheapest bulbs for naturalising or growing in quantity.

35 A Kaleidoscopic Garden

The idea was inspired by the kaleidoscope, an optical toy, the base of which is turned to form the gaily coloured pattern. In this garden one must move along a series of 'peep-holes' or windows to achieve the same effect.

The kaleidoscopic garden is summer flowering and a short-lived pleasure – say, from July to September or October in the northern hemisphere. For the rest of the year it should be hidde and it is therefore practical if it is surrounded by an interwoven fence upon which various plants can climb (see Plate 35). This type of fence is most suitable for a garden which is to be looked into – not a garden to be walked around in. Sitting on the benches outside the windows one can then enjoy the pleasant colour harmonies.

The arrangement should consist solely of really low, richly flowering annuals. Such a garden would be expensive in upkeep if one had to buy all the flowers as bedding out plants, but (fortunately) it is possible to sow many of them *in situ*. They merely need to be well thinned out as directed on the seed packets. If you have a greenhouse, many can be started there, even if it is not heated.

Use of coloured gravel
The kaleidoscopic garden need not remain without effect throughout the winter When the annuals are over one can, as in the early days of 'knot bedding', fill up the various sections with fine yellow, white and brick-coloured gravel or sand to make up the pattern – The soil should first be rolled lightly before scattering a thin layer of gravel over the sections, colour by colour. For even more contrast, damp peat dust can be sprinkled over the larger sections. Then on mild days you can enjoy the colour harmonies as much as during the summer; then, when the garden is to be replanted during the summer, all that needs doing is to blend the gravel and peat with the soil by means of a garden fork.

36 A Sunken Rockery

Here is an idea for a rockery without a rock garden, one to be placed in a sunny corner. It is not essential that the rockery is sunken in relation to the main garden level: one can raise the surroundings if there is too much soil – or can dig half-way down and surround the area with the soil thus removed. In this way one avoids removal of excess soil or the need to bring more soil to the site, both equally costly affairs today. Remember that good drainage in the planting areas is essential.

Dry stone walls and a 'tower'
Both are built of broken cement slabs and must have good foundations. For the 'tower' it is necessary to dig a 1-m (3-ft) deep hole, which is tightly packed with rubble. On this frost-free foundation, stones are placed to form this tall construction; good topsoil is then mixed with sand at the centre. The walls of this and the lower beds are of dry stone without mortar. Retaining walls of mortar are dull to look at and do not possess the character of dry stone walls. Considerable care is needed during construction so that each slab lies flat without wobbling.

It would be possible to incorporate a fireplace in the 'tower'. The plants would not suffer from a chimney in the centre, provided it was well insulated.

Several forms of shelter
To create shelter and privacy it would be possible to have a trimmed hedge surrounding the sunken area, or at least in the corner nearest the neighbours. Beech would be ideal here. But one could also imagine a free-growing arrangement of *Spiraea vanhouttei* or *Rosa rubiginosa*. The shelter shown in Plate 36 is more varied. The Chinese junipers are *Juniperus media* 'Pfitzerana' and 'Blaauw' as a background for the bench; the Japanese maple is *Acer palmatum* 'Atropurpureum' and the shrub rose *Rosa hugonis*.

In planting the cracks in the 'tower', a more artistic effect is created by arranging groups of the same plant varieties in several places and on the same walls; this is better than a wide variety of different plants.

Besides the plants suggested in Plate 36, one could also include a group of red valerian, *Centranthus ruber* 'Coccineus', and various types of *Potentilla fruticosa*.

Planting on the flat
The base should be planted with grass or pavement plants such as *Cotula squalida*, which can be trodden on, and which needs very

sandy, dry soil. Here and there solitary perennials can be planted at ground level. The base should maintain the character of a plain the whole time. In the example on the plate, some crazy paving has been laid and the following solitary perennials have been used: *Cytisus praecox* 'Hollandia', *Hosta fortunei*, *Primula denticulata*, *Sempervivum heuffelii*, *Verbascum densiflorum* and *Yucca filamentosa*. All these are hardy and would look wonderful in a close base of small pebbles from the beach, with perhaps *Kniphofia* 'Fireflame'.

37 A Herb Garden

It is difficult to say whether a herb garden has most justification for utility or as an element of design. Many herbs are beautiful with or without flowers and that a herb garden is scented makes it even more interesting. You should grow many different kinds of herbs even if they are not all used in the kitchen. The folklore of plants and their use makes them worth having just for the sake of cultural history. This applies to rue, *Ruta graveolens*, and hyssop, *Hyssopus officinalis*, which are not worth much as culinary items, but are very attractive plants.

Flagstones to encourage growth
The herb gardens of old monasteries were certainly laid out in a system of square beds with paths between, probably covered with gravel or flagstones. This type of garden has great aesthetic effect – a herb garden can be just as lovely to behold as a beautiful flowering garden. Ideally, one should enclose a herb garden with a hedge and possibly provide a seat. A lovely statue or a tasteful sundial would also be appropriate in this exclusive type of garden. Simple herbs require good, solid objects – not a modern birdbath or sundial made of plastic.

Paved paths strengthen the garden plan and, of course, make it easier to move about there. However, it has also been proved that plants grow much better between a system of paved paths than in open ground. It is nearly always damp under stones, so that roots gather there quite happily. Ordinary cement or composition stone flagstones can be also very attractive, but the effect is heightened if one uses cobbles or red bricks which create a subtler effect. In the example in Plate 37, grey granite setts have been used.

Annual and perennial herbs
Many herbs are perennials and can be bought at nurseries and garden centres. Examples are: sage, *Salvia officinalis*; thyme, *Thymus vulgaris*; wormwood, *Artemisia absinthium*; caraway, *Carum carvi*; sorrel, *Rumex acetosa*; mints, *Mentha spicata*, *M.crispa* and *M.piperita* (which one has to watch as they spread like wild-fire), lovage, *Levisticum officinale*; chives, *Allium schoenoprasum*; lavender, *Lavandula officinalis*; lemon balm, *Melissa officinalis*; tarragon, *Artemisa dracunculus*; and rosemary, *Rosmarinus officinalis*. Bay, *Laurus nobilis*, is a tree, but if pruned back can be grown among these perennials.

Annual herbs must be started from seed on a windowsill in the early spring, or sown directly in beds in April or May. Some of them may be found as seedlings at nurseries. Other notable annuals are: aniseed, *Pimpinella anisum*; fennel, *Foeniculum vulgare*; dill, *Anethum graveolens*; camomile, *Matricaria chamomilla*; marjoram, *Origanum majorana*; parsley, *Petroselinum crispum*; and summer savory, *Satureia hortensis*.

Watercress without running water
A particularly popular perennial herb, watercress, *Nasturtium officinale*, can be sown in the early spring. Tasty watercress can be grown in a shady position on bare soil without any ingenious devices using pools and running water, which most professionals consider necessary. Choose a half-shady position, place a 10–15cm (4–6in) thick layer of well-matured compost on top and rake it in well. Then sprinkle a packet of watercress seed over the bed, water it well using a can with a fine rose, and just wait several weeks, keeping it moist. Then suddenly, one day, you will notice tiny seedlings appearing which will grow very quickly. During the summer they will have formed a close, perfect carpet of watercress which can be harvested daily. The bed must never be allowed to dry out. Preferably it should be watered daily, but during damp periods it can look after itself. Watercress will re-establish itself from seeds which have survived the winter, if the bed is left undisturbed. If conditions make this impractical, use American land cress instead.

Ordinary cress, *Lepidium sativum*, which one only knows of as seedlings in boxes of cress, is really quite a large plant, which can be sown in the herb garden. When the plants are about 10cm (4in) tall, they can be cut and served like watercress. There is a much better harvest from cultivating cress in this way.

38   An Alpine Garden

Whether grown in large rock gardens or the small areas suggested in Plate 38, alpine or rock plants are often low, cushion-forming and richly flowering plants. Their blooming quite outshines the performance of other garden plants. Many of them are evergreen, as well as perennial. Most of them are easy to grow and plants can be found to suit all types of soil and positions in sun or shade. They tolerate most climates remarkably well. In their natural habitats these plants are used to quite harsh conditions, but they just will not tolerate standing dampness and they demand perfect drainage. A good rock garden has a thick layer of gravel and stones at the bottom, and above a layer of grit and soil. The actual soil for growth can be varied according to the needs of the plants. Some plants like an acid soil, while others prefer an alkali soil rich in lime. Most rock plants can be grown in a mixture of peat and topsoil mixed with gravel and small stones, using equal quantities of each.

Large stones should be placed between the plants, not to imitate a mountain landscape, but to create the vital local habitat. On the north side of large stones there is shade and a lower temperature than on the southern side. The temperature difference can be as much as 10°C (18°F), which means a great deal in the plant kingdom. The stones also help the warmth of the sun to penetrate the soil during the daytime and then lead the warmth up to the plants again during the night. During clear nights, plants growing in the open can have an internal temperature 5–6°C (9°F) below air temperatures on account of radiation; whereas plants which grow close up to stones can be warmer than the surrounding air.

The stones should be arranged neatly as it is never attractive to have large stones lying on top of the soil: one should not be able to imagine the real size, and their outlines should disappear into the ground. One could say that the rock work should merge with an imaginary mountain. Larger stones should have at least half their bulk underground, with small, loose stones scattered about to form an attractive arrangement.

In the rock garden there may be bare patches without vegetation, provided the soil is covered with stones of various sizes. The plants should cover adjoining areas. It is practical to make pockets amongst the stones so that each plant is separated; otherwise the task of weeding would be overwhelming. It is a good idea to let the larger stones act as stepping stones, so that one can move about the bed easily when working.

Alpine plants and special soils
Even if most alpine plants can be grown in a mixture of peat and topsoil mixed with gravel, there are varieties which require special soil and some gardening knowledge before they can be grown successfully. Generally speaking, it can be said that plants from woodland areas need soil which has been mixed with decaying leaves, pine needles and small twigs. Areas for growing heathers should have some acid heathland soil, which is fairly easily obtainable, otherwise the heathers must manage with coarse sand and peat. Chalk-loving plants, which include gentians and saxifrages, should have old, crushed rubble added to the soil, or limestone, or blackboard chalk broken into small and medium-sized pieces. Acid lovers, including the numerous dwarf rhododendrons, should be planted in a mixture of 1 part topsoil, 1 part coarse peat, 1 part leaf mould, and 2–3 parts small pieces of granite. The pH count should be 4 to 5; this can easily be tested with a modest and cheap kit. If the pH figure rises on account of too much watering with tap water, then once a year granulated or powdered sulphur can be added at 50–75gm per sq. m (about 2 oz per sq. yd).

Damp air
As mentioned previously, alpine plants do not enjoy standing dampness, but do prefer moist air around them, and during the growth period they benefit from water filtering down around their roots. That is why one sees sprinklers in the alpine beds of

botanical gardens; these provide a mild mist during the days when the weather is bright and dry.

Solitary plants

A rock garden should not only comprise low growing plants only. A small bush here and there will lend height, making the planting less flat and more natural. Varieties of broom are well suited for this purpose and if there is not room for the bush broom, *Cytisus praecox*, then one can use the small *C.decumbens* which only grows to a height of 20–30cm (8–12in). *Daphne mezereum* or the small *D.cneorum* will also lighten the effect. Dwarf varieties of common garden bushes such as berberis, potentilla and *Spiraea arguta* 'Compacta' are also suitable, but most appropriate of all, for the rockery, are the dwarf conifers, both in the creeping and pillar varieties of juniper, the dwarf fir *Picea glauca* 'Conica' and the Swiss mountain pine, *Pinus mugo*, which is found in several dwarf varieties.

39 A Water Garden

The vegetation along the banks of a stream or pond is rich and varied. The requirements for growth change within a short distance from deep water to dry land and this produces exciting plant life. One can recreate the same atmosphere in the garden in the form of a pond or stream as shown in Plate 39.

Materials for a garden pond

It can readily be seen from the illustration how the man-made stream and pond have been constructed. A watertight layer of cement laid underground maintains the depth of water at the right level. The cement is well protected from frost, but unfortunately not from cracks due to soil subsidence. One can save both money and frustration by substituting cement with a layer of heavy duty plastic sheeting, which can be bought at most garden centres and shops. Plastic sheeting is easy to work with as long as one remembers that it is resistant to tension, but not to pressure.

Make sure that there is a really smooth foundation of sand. A sharp stone quickly punctures the plastic when the weight of water presses the sheeting down on to the foundation. For a particularly strong but reasonably cheap pool, one can obtain pre-cast glass-fibre forms which are placed in appropriate excavations.

Water and marshland plants

Many of the plants available from nurseries can be seen growing wild in marshes and ponds. Observing the positions and depths in which they grow helps one to provide the right conditions at home in the garden. They can be grown in pots placed in wooden or plastic tubs, made watertight if necessary with a piece of heavy-duty black plastic sheeting. The natural depth of water will not be able to be kept with this means of cultivation, but the plants will manage for a while as long as there is water around the roots. One can learn a lot about water and marshland plants if one grows them in this way for a summer before attempting the larger pond or stream arrangement.

A choice of water plants

An area with water and streamside plants should be constructed so that the humidity in the soil decreases as the slope ascends. A precast pool give no possibility of moisture along the edge, unless one constantly allows it to overflow. Furthermore, the plants should be placed at the right depth for growth. This can vary from just a few centimetres to 40–50cm (say from 1–20in). Water lilies and water hawthorn can be placed in water of 30–50cm (12–20in) depth. The floating water plants also belong there, for example – frogbit, *Hydrocharis morsus-ranae*, water soldier, *Stratiotes aloides*, and water violet, *Hottonia palustris*.

Nearer the water's edge the following can be planted – Cat-tail, *Typha angustifolia*, arrowhead, *Sagittaria sagittifolia*, bog arum, *Calla palustris*, yellow flag, *Iris pseudacorus*, flowering rush, *Butomus umbellatus*, bog bean, *Menyanthes trifoliata*, marsh marigold (single or double), *Caltha palustris*, greater spearwort, *Ranunculus lingua*, marsh forget-me-not, *Myosotis scorpioides* and lady's smock, *Cardamine amara*. Before planting, the area should be cleared of perennial weeds; then the plants will be able to grow and multiply naturally amongst each other.

Higher up, but still in a damp position, one can plant all the perennials which do not do well in the too dry garden soil elsewhere. For example, globe flower, *Trollius hybridus*, creeping jenny, *Lysimachia nummularia*, *Ligularia clivorum*, garden meadow-sweet, *Astilbe arendsii*. Perennials such as day lilies (*hemerocallis*), hostas and *Rudbeckia nitida* much prefer a damp position. If space permits one can recommend acquiring the enormous *Gunnera manicata* which can grow up to 2m (6ft) tall with leaves like tea trays and flower heads almost like bunches of bananas! It needs effective protection during the winter, but it does grow well in various places in this country.

If one wishes to plant a single tree or bush along the water's edge the following would be suitable: the lovely weeping birch *Betula pendula*, dogwood, *Cornus alba*, or willow, *Salix purpurea*.

40 'Plant Sculptures'

A plant collector's garden is often a sad affair, as if a mania for collecting and an artistic nature seldom occur together. But in the garden here, the two ideas can be combined with the aid of a collection of unusual trees and shrubs.

These stand in low ground cover, which gives the possibility of collecting an assortment of, for example, bulbs and tubers, lilies, primulas, perennials for the shade, or possibly ground-cover plants.

Spacing the plants

A solitary plant is one which can – and should – stand alone. Note that all trees and shrubs in the garden have beautiful and distinctive shapes which entitle them to be placed at sufficient distances from each other. This allows them to be seen from all sides. If they are squeezed in among each other they lose their character and suffer accordingly. Evergreen trees and shrubs would lose their leaves or needles if they were overshadowed by other plants and would never be able to attain their natural beauty.

Distinctive 'architectural' plants are arranged in groups, but apart from each other, among low ground cover. Here, *Juniperus communis* 'Hibernica' and *Picea glauca* 'Conica' have been arranged in groups of three, though more or less could have been used in each group. This type of grouping can be used when pillar or pyramid-shaped trees are planted and slim trees would certainly benefit from the same treatment.

Ground cover

To cover the ground between 'plant sculptures' like this, grass or low ground-cover plants can be used, for example *Cotoneaster dammeri* and *C.horizontalis*, *Asarum europaeum*, and *Vinca minor*. A somewhat taller underplanting could be considered. For example in the illustration the junipers have been underplanted with the attractive, carpet-forming *J.communis* 'Repanda' reaching only 30–40cm (14–16in).

Accessibility of hedges

In the garden there is a path beside the hedges, allowing them to develop freely. It is pleasant to be able to walk around the plantation on the long path and enjoy the beautiful trees and shrubs. Common privet, *Ligustrum vulgare* 'Atrovirens', was used for the hedge here, but beech or yew could have been used, or a flowering plant such as *Berberis darwinii*.

41 A Miniature Garden

The Japanese art of gardening celebrates nature and landscape in a far more compact form than one is used to in the West. The Japanese also make use of symbols and aesthetic purity in a most characteristic way. Nevertheless, the artistic Japanese garden of studied elegance and purity makes a great impression on even the most unfamiliar eyes. The extension of world travel in recent years, and numerous new books on the subject, have brought the art of Japanese gardening nearer home. For example, there are a few Japanese gardens in England and one often comes across odd items from a Japanese garden – for instance an imported stone lamp, which can be bought at quite a reasonable price, the odd stepping stones in a pond, shingles with stepping stones between, and last but not least, bonsai trees.

Bonsai trees

The Japanese word *bonsai* means 'planted in a tray' and the trees in the miniature garden in Plate 41 are also planted in flat trays or bowls in the true Japanese manner. It taeks a long while to produce a true bonsai tree. Many Japanese bonsai trees are between 300–400 years old and they are hardly considered to be true bonsai until at least 100 years. A Scots pine cultivated as a bonsai tree has to be a true copy of a natural Scots pine, but with all measurements reduced to 1/10th or 1/20th of the norm. A tree which in its natural form would be 3–10m (10–32ft) tall, would be only 30–50cm (12–20in) tall as a bonsai tree, but with all proportions the same.

The art of bonsai
The art of bonsai culture requires a lot of gardening 'know-how'. Every shoot has to be bent and supported with copper wire for a long period until it has acquired the right shape. Pruning is done with a view to growth during the next 100 years! True bonsai trees are family treasures which have been started by distant relatives and kept going by the family gardeners through generations. The Bonsai trees on sale in this country are seldom more than 25 years old, but if well grown should begin to have the beauty and lilliputian size of the Japanese creation.

Older bonsai trees should be replanted every 3–4 years in the spring. One uses equal quantities of good topsoil, peat and fine gravel. The containers should have effective drainage at the bottom and the trees should be planted so that the roots are visible, like old trees in woods. The trays or bowls are usually 5–10cm (2–4in) deep and 15–35cm (6–14in) long and wide. The trees can remain out of doors throughout the year, because one cultivates the varieties which grow naturally in the local climate and will therefore withstand frost. (But during a hard winter it is advisable to place the trees near the window in a cold greenhouse or other light, cold but frost-free place.) Watering throughout the year must be minimal, but complete drying out should be avoided. Organic manure is preferable to artificial fertilizers, and this should be kept to the absolute minimum for existence.

Suitable trees
Much bonsai culture is based on pines, firs or larches, maples and occasionally birch. Almost any tree can be used but avoiding those with very large leaves like sycamore. One can 'cheat' a little with regard to age by starting bonsai culture with plants bought in their dwarf form. Thus one could obtain the naturally dwarf cypress *Chamaecyparis obtusa* 'Nana', and the dwarf pine,

Pinus mugo 'Mughus'. Many varieties of *Chamaecyparis* and *Thuja* are found in dwarf form as well as pines, firs and other conifers. However, the habit of these dwarfs is not ideal for true bonsai. The deciduous dawn cypress, *Metasequoia glyptostroboides*, although it is not found in a dwarf variety, is very suitable as a 'quick' bonsai.

To lend a little life to the stones in the bonsai garden the following have been planted here and there: *Calluna vulgaris* 'H. E. Beale', *Thymus serpyllum* 'Splendens' and the fescue grass *Festuca ovina* 'Glauca'.

42 Ornamental Grasses on the Lawn

The family of grasses is larger than any other group of plants, but it is the least used, if one disregards lawn grasses. It should be possible to create a garden composed solely of grasses as it would be attractive throughout the year. Even though many grasses are not evergreen, many of them look almost as attractive as winter 'skeletons' as they do in the summer.

A grass garden

The grass garden in Plate 42 is based on several beds in a corner of the lawn. Apart from being decorative, these beds create a space for a collection of amusing and attractive perennial grasses planted among large cobbles which contribute to the dramatic effect.

If one is smitten with collector's fever than the beds illustrated will not be enough. In that case, the ornamental grasses might be grown in an enclosed garden similar to the kaleidoscopic garden, lily garden or other specialized gardens illustrated in this book. When planting, one should follow the principles applied elsewhere in the garden – large areas with low ground-covering grasses in which tall grasses are placed as solitary plants.

Tall elephant grass

The Miscanthus tribe with its numerous varieties is among the most valuable of the perennial grasses. The tall panicles which are formed during the summer last throughout the winter, although they are dry and dead. A single specimen of elephant grass, *Miscanthus sacchariflorus* (sometimes listed as *M. sinensis*

194

'Giganteus') will grow to a height of up to 3m (10ft). *M.sinensis* varieties are smaller, but all of them are elegant and with their size they are a welcome variation in the grass garden.

There are many other types of grass to be found in nurseries suitable for every type of position, dry or damp, sunny or shady, so it is wise to find out about the conditions for growth before planting out in the garden.

Variations on the theme

There is no reason at all why a grass garden needs to be flat. Furthermore, one can vary the theme of the grass garden by not mowing the low grass – or certain areas of it – and letting it go to seed. Most tall grasses with drooping panicles are attractive and elegant. Normally one never sees the true appearance of lawn grasses. In such a lawn one can let hedgerow plants mix with the grass as already described for 'a meadow of flowers'. The meadow can be mown in the first week of June (Europe and North America) and then function for the rest of the summer as an ordinary lawn, though it will look rather yellow for the first fortnight after cutting. If you keep up the practice of a June cutting, you can have spring-flowering bulbs in the grass too. Alternatively, one can keep cutting the grass until June and then allowing it to grow, thus encouraging quite different, but equally attractive flora.

Dried grasses

The use of dried flowers and grasses in bouquets and wreaths is once again in fashion. Arranged tastefully and in the right containers such plants can be delightful indoors during the winter months. Most grasses suitable for this purpose are annuals and can be sown directly in the position for growth. The following varieties are usually available at a seed merchants and are most suitable: Greater quaking grass, *Briza maxima*, squirrel-tail grass, *Hordeum jubatum*, hare's tail, *Lagurus ovatus*, *Setaria italica*, and common maize, *Zea mays*. Barley, oats and corn are also suitable.

43 A Butterfly Sanctuary

It is quite an easy task to arrange one's garden so that it becomes a sanctuary for butterflies, bees and other attractive insects – and the garden will be even prettier since the butterflies' favourites are nearly all beautiful plants. Butterflies only come to plants whose flowers exude nectar, in other words the ones on which bees also feed. However, there are many garden flowers which have neither scent nor nectar.

For the butterfly sanctuary shown in Plate 43, a selection of shrubs and perennials has been chosen which is particularly attractive to butterflies. Besides those varieties illustrated, many other late-flowering, pollen-filled flowers are good 'butterfly magnets', for example helianthemums, *Hyssopus officinalis*, *Origanum vulgare*, *Reseda odorata* (mignonette) and *Sedum spectabile*. The early-flowering plants are really for the bees only.

44 Tropical Lushness for Summer

Owners of new gardens are often upset, because plants seem to grow so slowly. It takes at least four years before a garden grows up moderately in size, and even longer before the plant arrangements can provide privacy. Yet there are a number of plants which can grow very tall or produce lush ground within a single summer. Unfortunately, most of them are annuals and die with the first night frost. In conjunction with light fencing, it is possible to make a corner of the garden look 'tropical' with the aid of such plants. Most shown in Plate 44 are annuals: *Musa ensete* is an ornamental banana which can be wintered indoors. A number of permanent plants ensures that this particular corner of the garden is not bare during the winter. The bamboo fencing, wooden table, bench and 'paving' all contribute to the tropical illusion.

45 Green Cubism

There is nothing peculiar or fastidious about a well trimmed hedge, either as a garden boundary, or around an independent space in a garden. One can see several examples of the latter in this book. In the illustration the trimmed hedge is not just a fence, but also acts as a shape in the garden picture. Every garden is made up of shapes, even a garden that consists entirely of trees and shrubs grown naturally; thus it is not such a great step to the cubist garden. People with an artistic sense or who enjoy beautiful shapes, will be able to appreciate these features in both the natural garden and the formal cubist one.

Cubism as an integral feature

It is not intended that the whole garden should consist of topiary, as one would soon tire of looking at it and nothing else. As a feature it is an excellent idea, just as a scented garden, herb garden or butterfly sanctuary are features which make for a richer life around the house.

The trimmed shapes are in sharp contrast to Nature's graceful and irregular forms. A cubist garden has many faces. In grey weather and rain, the colours are intense – and in sunshine it is the shadows which create endless variation. A whole new world can be seen when snow or hard frost settles on the trimmed globes, cones or pyramids.

Shaping hedge plants

Any plant which has the characteristics demanded by an ordinary trimmed hedge is also suitable for topiary; so the selection is quite large. Even trees can be considered, like globe-acacias, rowans and plane trees.

For smaller and more detailed shapes box and yew are best suited; others are listed in Plate 45. Apart from *Fagus silvatica*, beech, and *Carpinus betulus*, hornbeam, the following can be recommended too: *Cornus mas*, Cornelian cherry, *Lonicera pileata*, honeysuckle privet, *Pyracantha coccinea*, firethorn, and *Ribes alpinum*, mountain currant. Among plants which have a good shape from nature's own hand is *Thuja occidentalis* 'Fastigiata', which, having a single trunk, does not break in the snow. A bigger conifer for a more massive effect is Leyland cypress, *Cupressocyparis leylandii*; it has a golden form called 'Castle-wellan'.

46 An Exotic Back Garden

It is quite wrong to think that an enclosed garden just outside the living room windows would be oppressive. On the contrary, there is nothing more pleasant than to look out upon a small world of flowering perennials, climbing plants and exotic looking trees and bushes. There is nothing at all odd about the lawn being hidden from the living room. After all, one can enjoy the lawn when walking around the garden. When all is said and done, a garden reckons to provide experiences and pleasant sitting-out places and should not be arranged just to show friends how large a plot one owns!

Year-long interest
An enclosed garden should contain plants of all-year-round appeal. They do not have to be evergreen, but can include plants that either have an interesting branch formation, such as *Rhus typhina* 'Laciniata', or have pretty flowerheads which remain attractive even throughout the winter, like *Achillea filipendulina* 'Coronation Gold', *Sedum spectabile* 'Autumn Joy', and the tall, decorative elephant grass, *Miscanthus sacchariflorus*, whose compact, bamboo-like top stands like a pillar and sways in the wind until the new shoots appear in the spring. How dull it is to go into gardens where everything that has faded has been cut off at ground level when the leaves fall!

In an *enclosed* back garden, half or more of the area should be paved and if there are lush plants, one does not really notice the paving stones. Of course the paving should have a restful character and not be laid in a contrived pattern which captures all the attention, or worst of all, consist of paving stones of two different colours laid in a misguided attempt to be 'artistic'. Even the lushest plant arrangement could not help this disaster

Choice of exotic plants
For one reason or another many plants have an exotic appearance, so the choice is quite wide. Beside the plants shown in Plate 46, others worth considering are *Hosta glauca*, *Macleaya cordata* 'Coral Plume', plume poppy, *Helianthus salicifolius*, perennial sunflower, hemerocallis or day lilies, climbing *Hydrangea petiolaris* and *Aristolochia durior*, Dutchman's pipe. They all have vigorous growth rates which will give character to any back garden of this type.

47 A Scented Back Garden

Plants with a pleasant scent should be collected in a warm, enclosed garden just outside the living room door, so that on windless days one can leave the door open and be aware of the delicate scent right inside the rooms. Just think of the intoxicating cherry pie, mock orange and honeysuckle.

In the back garden illustrated in Plate 47, there will be a delicate scent from early spring to late summer. The early *Viola odorata* is the first to produce its sweet-scented blossom. Then it is followed by wallflowers, lilies-of-the-valley, and early Dutch honeysuckle. Then from mid-summer and into late autumn there will be lilacs (syringa), sweet rocket, *Hesperis matronalis*, mock oranges (philadelphus), *Rosa rubiginosa* 'Lady Penzance', lavender, and Madonna lily, *Lilium candidum*, all of which have a delightful perfume in the green surroundings.

In the colour plate the back garden has been given a soft green carpet of grass with stepping stones where the grass is most likely to be down-trodden. One could also imagine a raised scented garden with the beds raised about 70cm (27in) and supported by boulders or cobblestones. Then you could walk about and delight in the lovely scents even more closely. Near the wall facing the road, a couple of Serbian spruce, *Picea omorika*, have been planted with a couple of juniper bushes, *Juniperus communis* 'Hibernica' and 'Repanda', and another mock orange; and behind the enclosed garden, a silver spruce, *Abies nobilis* 'Glauca'.

Delicately scented plants

Among other shrubs worth mentioning are *Viburnum fragrans*, which begins flowering as early as winter, the late spring-flowering scented snowball tree, *Viburnum burkwoodii*, and *Daphne mezereum* which flowers with the first violets. Hyacinths and cherry pie (the latter is kept as a pot plant throughout the winter) also belong among strongly-scented plants. Mignonette, *Reseda odorata*, stocks and perennial phlox must not be omitted from the scented garden, and the very hardy yellow rose 'Chinatown' should not be forgotten either as it is reckoned among the most strongly-scented roses. One could also grow the well named geranium-pink 'Fragrant Cloud'.

Herbs are also types of scented plants. One could easily imagine a combined herb and scented garden, especially as so many herbs are very attractive.

You could also try a common elderberry bush. Some people may think that this belongs to the countryside; but one could hardly find a prettier or more hardy bush, with scented flowers, than the elder. Of course, it also provides attractive fruit which can be made into a good red wine.

48 Colour Gardens

The advantage of a large garden is that it can be divided into smaller sections, so that one can walk from one effect to the next. The two flower gardens with carefully blended shades shown in Plate 48 are amusing inside, but also useful in that the surrounding hedges lend character to the garden outside.

A consistent choice of colour
The arrangements are kept within the blue, mauve and pink, and the yellow, orange and red shades respectively, following the colour principles outlined elsewhere in this book. In both cases perennials and annuals have been included in the selection of plants.

The colour combinations in the flower garden to the left will be cool and comfortable on a still, hot summer's day when the sun beats down on the south-facing terrace in front of the house. Later, when the sun sends its last rays into the garden and the air becomes cooler, one can move into the flower garden on the right where all the brightly-coloured 'hot' flowers are grouped together.

It is obvious that the choice of colour must be consistent. Furniture, garden umbrellas, cushions, covers and anything else which is brought into the garden must not mar the effect. The paving should be of a restful character and neutral colour and one should avoid patterns which distract the eye. Notice how the dark paving stones, used here, strongly emphasize the colours of the flowers.

Well-trimmed hedges
The hedges form a compact, green frame which by their very
shape produce a sculptured effect. *Lonicera nitida* or thuja could
be used and they should be kept closely trimmed. It is precisely
these sharp lines which emphasize the flower garden's more
relaxed and colourful interior.

An enclosed flower garden would also be very suitable for
framing a collection of dahlias which are normally a little too
vivid amongst the garden's other flowers.

49 A Garden of 'Separate Rooms'

No garden should be able to be capable of being seen at a single
glance. There should be hidden corners that encourage one to
explore and the size of the garden plays only a small part in this.
It is the division that makes the idea exciting. Even the small
garden of a terraced house can easily contain a mass of details.
Unfortunately, it is often a problem for the owner to gather the
various details into the harmonious entity shown in Plate 49.

Against the wall of the house there is a *Cotoneaster salicifolius
floccosus* (1 on the plate), *Buddleia davidii* 'Magnifica' (2) and
Clematis 'The President' (3), and up the fence to the right a
Viburnum rhytidophyllum (4) underplanted with St. John's wort,
Hypericum calycinum (5). A blue *Wisteria sinensis* and a yellow
honeysuckle, *Lonicera tellmanniana*, would also have been pretty
on the house wall and fence, respectively.

In the 'front room' along the path around the garden are
woodland flowers such as *Lilium martagon*, *L.regale* and *L.speciosum*
(6–8), and around them *Primula bulleyana*, *P.florindae* and *P.veris*
(9–11). Among the lilies, ferns and lilies-of-the-valley can be
planted; and among the primulas, spring bulbs. A *Clematis* 'Jack-
manii' would also look well against the fence.

In the next 'room', apart from different varieties of *Phlox
paniculata*, one is greeted by brightly-coloured blue, yellow and
red perennials like *Aster amellus* 'Blue King' (13), *Chrysanthemum
coccineum* 'Scarlet Glow' (14) and *Helenium* 'The Bishop' (15).
Geum 'Mrs. Bradshaw', delphiniums and *Rudbeckia speciosa* would
have been suitable too. Some tall, late-flowering tulips could

be planted amongst the phlox, just as a *Clematis* 'Ville de Lyon' would also have looked attractive against the fence. In the farthest corner of the garden a couple of dark green bushes have been planted; on the right, a holly, *Ilex aquifolium* (16) and on the left a yew, *Taxus baccata* (17).

Besides the shade-loving plants – ivy, asarabacca and periwinkle – at the bottom of the garden the yellow bamboo, *Sinarundinaria murielae* (21) has been planted, and close to it the delicate, pale *Cercidiphyllum japonicum* (22). A red and yellow honeysuckle, *Lonicera henryi*, underplanted with Solomon's seal, *Polygonatum multiflorum*, would be most suitable up against the interwoven fence.

Continuing around the garden, in the last two 'rooms', there are mixed hybrid tea roses (23), and acid-loving plants such as rhododendrons and heathers. These could include *Rhododendron luteum* (24), *R. praecox* (25), **Daphne** *mezereum* (26) underplanted with varieties of *Calluna vulgaris* (27) and *Erica carnea* (28); *Rhododendron catawbiense* 'Album' (29) and the hardy hybrids 'Pink Pearl' and 'Purple Splendour' (3). Against the interwoven fence, large-flowered climbing roses could be planted, such as 'Danse du Feu', 'Schoolgirl' and 'High Noon'. The daphne could be substituted with a dainty *Magnolia stellata*.

Up against the fence, along the edge of the last two 'rooms', *Clematis montana* 'Rubens' (31) and the large-flowered 'Nelly Moser' (33) have been grown, underplanted with *Cotoneaster dammeri* (32) and *C. horizontalis* (34), respectively.

The garden described here will take a long time to walk around. Here and there, a few seats have been carefully placed to catch the morning, afternoon and evening sunshine. One could create a wonderful scene by illuminating the garden with some low-powered spotlights.

Two different suggestions

In the plan which has just been considered, the garden has been split up with the aid of interwoven fences that have been placed at right angles to the boundary. The same effect could have been achieved with clipped hedges, apart from the fact that fences provide room for some interesting climbing plants and do not have any water-seeking root systems, so that one is able to plant close to the woodwork. Small gardens should always be surrounded by fences because the roots of hedges extend a long way on either side.

One could easily imagine the grass substituted with different ground-cover plants, each in large expanses of up to several square metres. Among these, graceful flowering shrubs, unusual evergreens and groups of bulbs could be grown – all sufficient distance apart to allow every detail to be clearly emphasized. But however the garden is arranged, every bit of soil must be covered with vegetation. A couple of graceful trees should be introduced to lend height and produce fascinating shadow effects. *Cercidiphyllum japonicum*, *Amelanchier laevis*, *Rhus typhina*, *Magnolia soulangiana* and *Gleditsia triacanthos* are all good examples of trees which do not grow particularly large.

50 Roses and Lilies

If a gardener wishes to choose a couple of specialities from the wide variety of flowering plants, one could hardly recommend two better families than roses and lilies. Nowadays there is a tremendously wide variety of both, with new ones appearing each year.

Roses and lilies grown separately
Here is a scheme for roses planted in small beds of their own with 3–5 plants of the same variety in each bed. The bushes are kept 25–40cm (10–16in) apart according to the growth and size of the particular variety. For ground cover or for interplanting, one can use low evergreen plants or low annuals among which early spring bulbs can be grown.

Lilies are grown in special beds too, where they can be grown singly or in clusters of 3–5 plants of each variety. Greedy shrubs or perennials must not be used for interplanting; instead use only hardy, shade-loving plants such as anemones, ferns, lilies-of-the-valley and early spring bulbs.

While ordinary soil is fine for roses, it is better to use good garden soil which has been dug 2 spits deep with the possible addition of a little gravel, lilies need a very porous soil rich in organic matter and mixed with good decaying leaf mould or compost.

51 Colour Perspective

In earlier times, landscape designers attempted to make gardens seem larger and richer in contents – an illusion made possible by false perspective. Set pieces and even mirrors were used to create artificial atmospheres with the aid of pale or dark plant arrangements, grottos, pagodas, 'ruins' and other theatrical effects.

When planning a modern garden it is essential to consider its purpose first and foremost – but naturally any garden should at the same time be both beautiful and full of interest. Here, a knowledge of both linear and colour perspective is useful, provided it is used with discretion. In paintings the use of such perspective will make pure, bright colours such as red, yellow and blue appear closer than the pale delicate colours such as mauve, pale blue and pale pink. This phenomenon can be used to advantage in a garden to create an effect of greater size and depth. All that is required is to plant flowers according to 'colour perspective'.

Brightly coloured flowers should be placed in the foreground; the woodland's pale, graceful flowers can be scattered in groups among dark, evergreen bushes in the background to give depth. For the same reason, plants with large, characteristic leaves such as *Corydalis lutea*, *Dicentra spectabilis*, *Polygonatum multiflorum* and ferns should be placed in the background. The decorated, vertical posts in Plate 51 will heighten the illusion and make the garden appear even larger when viewed from the terrace. They will also minimise the effect of the boundary hedges.

52 A Rhododendron Garden

In a sufficiently large area of acid soil, the rhododendron family with its almost innumerable species and varieties is one of the best choices in which to specialise. The scope is tremendous as the family includes giants and dwarfs with many intermediate sizes, deciduous and evergreen, with a wonderful range of colours. In Europe and North America blooms appear from January through to early July. Blossom time in the rhododendron bed can of course be extended with all types of bulbs from early spring to the late summer lilies. There are also numerous ground cover plants which prefer acid soil. Here we will just mention the primula family which has varieties flowering from spring to late summer and moreover would be another excellent plant in which to specialise.

Acid soil for humus

The term 'acid-soil plants' really covers only half the demands which rhododendrons make with regard to soil. Chemically speaking, one can make many types of soil acid, without necessarily making it suitable for cultivating rhododendrons. If one planted acid-lovers in compact clay, they would soon become pale and lose their strength even though one kept the pH level sufficiently low. Technically speaking, it would be better to call acid-soil-loving plants 'raw-humus-loving plants'. Raw humus is vegetable matter in a state of slow decomposition. This produces a very light, porous soil with plenty of oxygen for the plant roots. Oxygen is one of the most important factors for the growth of acid-loving plants; the pH level should be 4·0–5·0, and the depth of soil should be at least 50–60cm (20–24in). Admittedly rhododendron roots do not go down particularly far, but it has been known for damaging substances such as calcium to travel up through the earth beneath the bed of acid soil. It is therefore necessary to have a layer which acts as a buffer under the plants. The bed of acid soil should be well-drained, as standing winter dampness is fatal to the plants. If there is no natural drainage through the subsoil one must dig some holes deep enough to allow the water to escape, for excess must be removed. These holes should be filled in with gravel and stones.

   Acid soil can be mixed as follows:

> 1 part topsoil,
> 1 part coarse peat,
> 1 part good leaf mould,
> ½ part pine needles,
> 2–3 parts fine gravel.

It would be wise to test the mixture with a soil-testing kit before planting.

Moving rhododendrons

Rhododendrons have a compact root system and can be moved without causing damage. Moreover, they can be planted throughout the year, even when in bloom. One should not plant them any deeper than they were before. It is wise to place a 10–15cm (4—6in) deep layer of leaves in between the rhododendrons each year to feed the soil. Should the root clump have become dry during transport, it should be placed in a bucket of water for an hour before planting out. The dry peat-like substance which forms the root clump is water-resistant and it can take weeks before it is softened by the dampness of the soil. Plants can die of thirst after planting out in spite of having a hose on them for an hour each day!

Watering

Preferably, rhododendrons and other acid-lovers should be watered with rain water, but ordinary tap water, even if it is hard, is better than allowing them to dry out. They cannot withstand any drying out of the root. Once the leaves begin to curl up and hang, the plant is seriously damaged and will have great difficulty in recovering.

Other requirements

Most acid-lovers, including rhododendrons, do not like rich soil and so they must be fed sparingly. An important source of nourishment is the layer of leaves that should be scattered around the plants annually. In addition, one can use 40–50gm (about 1½oz) balanced fertilizer and 20–30gm ammonium sulphate per sq. m (about ½oz per sq. yd) each year, but it is advisable to divide this amount and apply it several times during the season.

Ammonium sulphate cannot be used to reduce the pH level as many people believe. If the pH level is too high, one has to use granulated or powdered sulphur – 50–75gm per sq. m .(about 2oz per sq. yd) should be sufficient. The sulphur is converted gradually to sulphuric acid and this slowly reduces the pH level.

Traces of iron and manganese are found in sufficient quantity in acid soil. However should these substances be lacking, the leaves will become pale, possibly with dark green veins. This might also be an indication that the pH level has risen. If this occurs, the plants should be treated with a sequestrene compound according to the instructions on the package.

Seed formation
When rhododendrons have finished flowering, one should pinch out the flower-heads carefully. If the seeds are allowed to develop, they will take the strength from the plant which would otherwise have gone into building up the plant. Pruning should only be undertaken if the plant has become too large or if a branch is in the way. Healthy plants normally sprout readily after pruning, which should preferably be done in March or April.

53 A Mirror of Water

One of the old manor garden's most attractive features was the ornamental pool framed with trees, shrubs and perennials with outstanding foliage. Many pools were of a considerable size, but in today's gardens one can manage splendidly with a pond of 1 × 2m (3 × 6ft), or one of 1½ × 10m (5 × 32ft) as illustrated in Plate 53. In either case, the depth need only be 20–30cm (8–12in). Whether the pool be made of concrete, plastic sheeting or glass fibre its ability to reflect will be increased if one paints the interior black with bituminous paint or a plastic substance, which will also help to make the pool watertight. Remember to allow the colouring to dry thoroughly before filling the pool with water.

Plants for beautiful reflections
The mirror effect of a pool is fascinating in dull or sunny weather. The nearby plants move in the slightest breeze which ruffles the water. Along the edge of the pool, and close to it, trees, shrubs and different perennials with particularly attractive leaves should be planted. Flowers too appear fascinating when reflected in the water. The deciduous varieties of rhododendron would look lovely, with their bright yellow, orange and red flowers in the early summer. They must be supported by other plants, so that there is something throughout the year.

Besides the trees and shrubs listed in Plate 53, a couple of evergreens should not be missing from the immediate surroundings. It could be, for example, a couple of tall, slim Serbian spruce, *Picea omorika*, and *Viburnum burkwoodii* or *V.rhytidophyllum*. The last two flower in the early summer. The selection of perennials suggested could easily be supplemented with decorative rhubarb, *Rheum palmatum*, and day lilies, hemerocallis, the latter having both beautiful leaves and flowers.

In addition to providing a peaceful background, the foreground 'wings' of the clipped yew hedge limit the view over the pool and make it all the more exciting to look out upon through the opening. Limiting a view by framing it produces one of the most striking effects in the art of gardening.

The ornamental pool's worst enemies are algae and duckweed, but they can be eradicated with a strong dose of copper sulphate, since there is no fish or plant life to worry about. Start with a solution of 5gm copper sulphate per litre of water (about $\frac{3}{4}$oz per gallon), increasing the dose if necessary.

54 Fruit as a Feature

Many varieties of fruit can be grown in a limited area and if this is sunny and sheltered, it is possible to grow an assortment that would normally be difficult in the open garden of a cooler climate. This is particularly true of pears. The cultivation of espaliered fruit trees (or other trained forms) does make for a little more work because the trees must be pruned and sprayed if the quality is to be perfect and, of course, a very strong, rigid framework of wood with horizontal framing wires is essential. Besides apples, pears, apricots, plums and peaches, cherries and grapes can be trained, and if one has room, red and blackcurrant bushes are equally suitable for growing as espaliers or multiple cordons.

A warmer climate in such a situation can tempt early blossom and there can be a risk of damage from frost on clear nights. Sheets of hessian, old sacking or similar material must be hung over the rows, perhaps on a wooden framework.

While it is possible to train one's own trees from 'maidens', time is saved by buying partly trained trees. They should always be on dwarfing rootstocks.

Packing them in
Even more varieties can be grown in a limited space by planting single-stemmed cordon trees. These go in about 70cm (about 2ft) apart, though plums and cherries need 90cm (3ft). The stems are tied securely to the training wires at an angle of 45—60 degrees to the ground. The side shoots are kept very small by 'spur-pruning' both in summer and in late winter.

55 A 'Vitamin Grove' of Fruit and Vegetables

It is unusual to see fruit trees and bushes planted in a lawn, but the effect can be just as attractive as with ornamental varieties and bushes. There is, of course, more work entailed in looking after a lawn planted with trees and shrubs. In the early stages each tree must have a ring of bare earth around it, since grass has a surprisingly restricting effect on growth. This entails trimming the grass around each little bed. Later, when the trees are more mature, grass can be allowed right up to the trunk: this curtails growth, encourages fruiting, and looks more attractive. This grass will need periodic trimming with shears.

Add plenty of nitrogen
Nitrogen is the main food chemical 'stolen' by the grass roots before it seeps down to the deeper-lying tree roots. To overcome this, distribute a nitrogenous fertilizer more often and in larger quantities than usual. It is difficult to give general rules: if the trees do not develop healthy, dark leaves but are pale and sickly, rush out with a bag of fertilizer!

Apart from the artistic effect, grass under fruit trees has the advantage that windfalls are not damaged.

Living off the garden
People who think that one should grow one's own fruit and vegetables have worked out that one needs approximately 1 sq. m (11 sq. ft) per person per day to provide complete nutritional requirements, provided that one can store surpluses for the winter. This calculation is for vegetarians; meat-eaters can manage with somewhat less. Remember that fruit and vegetables provide many vitamins.

Good varieties of fruit
Besides all the 'regular' fruits suggested in general terms, others
with special value in making wine, syrups, jelly and herbal
remedies could include large-hipped roses, for example *Rosa
rugosa*, sea buckthorn, *Hippophaë rhamnoides*, Cornelian cherry,
Cornus mas, elder, *Sambucus nigra*, crab apples like 'John Downie',
and the little Japanese quince *Chaenomeles japonica*. On very acid
soils the large-fruited blueberry, *Vaccinium corymbosum*, is a valuable plant, which will not grow in ordinary soil.

56   A Seaside Holiday House

One cannot apply town garden principles to the seaside garden.
Here the various parts of a garden – such as sitting-out areas,
barbecue area, sun-trap, and the house itself – should merge
into the landscape as unobtrusively as possible. Use pebbles
instead of cement paving stones; interwoven willow instead of
wooden fences; free-growing shrubs and groups of perennials
instead of close-clipped hedges and formal flower beds. Try to
avoid the temptation of putting up an imitation well without
water, a windmill decorated with shells or an old car tyre full of
geraniums. It could be that your neighbours have good taste!

Planning
A seaside garden should have 100% privacy. It is ideal if the
garden has several individual clearings, the whole surrounded by
closely planted trees and bushes which extend to the boundary.
Even quite a small seaside plot can be interesting if you can
walk about between the clearings along narrow grass paths,
without being able to notice that you are in an area with hundreds
of houses. In a lot of seaside gardens the arrangement consists
of a single row of shrubs or conifers along the boundary, with
grass elsewhere. How could one possibly relax and feel in contact
with nature in such a garden?

Planting
As pointed out in Plate 56, many plants will not tolerate seaside
conditions, but there are plenty which can tolerate sea spray and
high winds. Try to discover plants which 'belong' at the coast.

Besides those recommended in Plate 58 other trees and shrubs which thrive in poor, sandy, windswept soil are *Amelanchier laevis*, *Berberis thunbergii*, *Crataegus crus-galli* and the snowberries, *Symphoricarpos*. Species roses form good hedging, for example *Rosa rugosa* or *R.rubiginosa*, but one could use *Berberis verruculosa* or *Spiraea vanhouttei* on the boundary equally well.

57   A Sunken Sun-trap

This is particularly effective as part of the seaside garden and is very important here because it will contribute greatly to the use of the garden when gusty winds make life on the beach impossible. But it could be an asset in any family garden.

For the first few years, until the plant groupings have matured, one can create shelter by erecting some cheap straw mats on wooden posts. Corrugated plastic windbreaks in bright colours should be avoided.

58   A Patio with a Fireplace

Summer evenings can often be too chilly to allow one to sit out of doors. One can use an infra-red electric heater to warm up the sitting-out area, but how much more attractive is an open fire. Fortunately, it is easy to arrange an open fireplace on a patio, where a screen can preserve the heat and create a cosy corner in the garden for the whole family to sit in during peaceful summer evenings.

Planning and planting around the fireplace
The fireplace can be built of different types of stone, but the simplest plan is to buy a ready-made cast-iron fireplace and arrange it in conjunction with a circular fence as shown in Plate 58. The circular shape is arrived at by attaching two or three horizontal, galvanised iron banks to a row of impregnated wooden support posts, and fixing to these horizontals the correct number of spruce posts without bark. Alternatively, if the circular shape proves too difficult, one can form a many-sided screen consisting of a lot of small ready-made screens of larchlap or interwoven wood.

The 'floor' of the fireplace area should perhaps have a somewhat primitive appearance, so ordinary cement paving stones are best avoided. An attractive, inexpensive covering is obtained by placing a number of flat pieces of granite or boulders at quite a distance from each other and filling in the gaps with egg-sized pebbles laid in a thin layer of dry cement. Moss or pearlwort will grow into the cracks and produce an even more pleasing appearance.

The area around the fireplace and its screen should harmonise with its surroundings. One could use a group of informal trees, both conifers and deciduous, as shown in the illustration.

59 A Cottage Garden

The cottage garden belongs among our cultural souvenirs just as much as the timbered, thatched cottages themselves, which seem to be part and parcel of the European landscape. All too often one sees a lot of money being spent on restoring the building in the old style, while the garden is ruined by the introduction of cement paving, imitation wells, plastic gnomes and far too sophisticated plants to mix with the old-fashioned roses, hollyhocks and fruit trees. Gardens have their periods in the same way as architecture.

The original scheme
The house and garden together should continue to form an attractive part of the landscape. Instead of altering the whole character of the garden, one should try to keep to the original plan as far as possible. Do not let all the pollarded poplars and willows, bent old fruit trees, elderberry bushes, honeysuckle, broad box hedges and old-fashioned scented roses be victims of the saw. With appropriate pruning and the addition of fresh soil, most of them can usually be rejuvenated.

If it is necessary to add to the original plants, choose others to blend with them. Old-fashioned roses – or newer ones with the old-fashioned look like 'Joybells' and 'Constance Spry' – are ideal in such settings, together with mock orange (philadelphus), *Daphne mezereum* and lavender. The last would be in keeping as a hedge around the rose bed. Beneath the old fruit trees there should be masses of crocuses, scillas, snowdrops and narcissi. Dame's Violet, *Hesperis matronalis*, and its relation *H.tristis*, violets, lilies-of-the-valley, honesty and foxgloves can be allowed to grow in peace and multiply under the elder trees.

Perennials

The old-fashioned garden often has large clumps of hardy, long-lived perennials, such as easily grown varieties of golden rod, phlox, michaelmas daisy and *Rudbeckia nitida*, all of which flower over a long period and are good for cutting. Often the original clump has never been divided and it has spread over a whole square metre. Actually, it is most attractive just like that and one should try to preserve such an old clump when possible. Technically speaking, it would probably be better to divide and replant in fresh soil once in a while, but the charm of the cottage garden with its large clumps of perennials and bare soil between would be lost if one became too professional.

Natural materials for paths and fences

Daisies should be allowed to remain in the lawn and instead of cement-paved paths one should have narrow paths of cobble-stones, hard-fired bricks or gravel. A herb garden with small, square beds edged with red bricks could easily blend with the rural scenery. Should it be necessary to fence the property along the public road, it would be most attractive in the form of a rockery wall of large boulders. Here, hardy unpretentious flowers such as *Campanula portenschlagiana*, erigerons, *aubrieta*, *Cerastium tomentosum* and pinks are suitable.

Velvet-gloved 'restoration'

The example in Plate 59 shows how one might recreate a cottage garden in the modern idiom, provided great care is taken. The elderberry tree at the corner of the house and the hollyhocks against the walls have been kept from the original plan layout, while the round beds amongst the cobblestones and grass have been newly arranged and planted with perennials and roses. The old double peony *Paeonia officinalis* 'Rubra plena' is a typical cottage flower, like the shasta daisy *Chrysanthemum maximum* 'Universal'. Other suitable plants are roses like 'Allgold' and

213

'Peace', *Aubrieta* 'Dr. Mules', *Campanula carpatica*, *Vinca minor*, *Aster amellus* 'Blue King', *Papaver orientale* varieties and *Helenium* 'Moerheim Beauty'. These are a few of the flowers that have that certain old-fashioned feeling.

60 A Moorland Garden

Heather appears in moorland areas with sandy soils where trees are unable to grow, but it is in fact only one stage of nature's changing vegetation. In Scotland, where the Forestry Commission has planted so many new coniferous trees, the enormous patches of heather are becoming fewer and fewer. The Highland crofters used to use heather for fuel, mattresses and thatching their cottages, etc. The animals on the farm ate the seedling trees and other 'weeds' and occasionally a heath fire would do a more thorough job of weeding for the farmer, and the heather would grow with renewed vigour in clean soil. To maintain heather in a moorland area, one has to weed thoroughly or it will revert naturally to a wooded area.

Plant pine, fir and juniper
Moorland plants are used to poor, sandy soil and coniferous trees are adapted for those conditions. They grow more compact and elegant in shape than when planted in good quality topsoil which causes them to become straggly and produce too many shoots. Do not plant unusual or exotic dwarf conifers on a moorland plot as they would not merge with the surrounding landscape. Keep to Beach pine, *Pinus contorta*, Scots pine, *P.sylvestris*, Austrian pine, *P.nigra*, white spruce, *Picea glauca* and Sitka spruce, *P.sitchensis*. Juniper is another typical plant of poor soils. Many people only recognise the upright variety of juniper which forms slim, column-shaped trees, but the forms of juniper range from low ground cover to bush shape and finally column-shaped plants. In general, it is the bushy varieties that are most appropriate in a moorland garden, such as *Juniperus communis*, *J.virginiana*, *J.chinensis* and the flattish *J.horizontalis*.

Difficulties with heather
Heather is the typical moorland plant and will only grow where

it wants to grow! It is no use taking up plants and expecting them to grow; it is far better to let the heather sow itself by placing seed-bearing twigs of heather on top of the soil, provided it is sandy and acid – otherwise it will be a hopeless task. Nurseries have a wide selection of heathers, almost suggesting that it would be easy to start one's own private heath. The easiest types to grow are the ericas, including the bell and Cornish heaths. Wild heather or ling, *Calluna vulgaris*, also has numerous garden forms.

Moorland shrubs
Amelanchier laevis, Cytisus praecox and *Caragana arborescens* are largish hardy shrubs which would not spoil the natural landscape. Small species rhododendrons would also grow well in sheltered spots. Among roses one should select species which preserve their 'uncultured' appearance, like *Rosa pimpinellifolia, R.rubrifolia* and *R.rugosa*. One should avoid ordinary hybrid tea roses and other brightly coloured plants such as dahlia or Japanese cherry. It is of the utmost importance to maintain and respect the landscape's original character; a moorland plot is not at all ideal for the flower-garden enthusiast.

61 The Mountains as Neighbours

What was said about the garden of the moorland holiday house is equally true for a garden among mountains. Here again, spruces, pines, firs and junipers give a natural effect, which can be added to with low alpine plants. If a small kitchen garden is required, it could be surrounded by a dry stone wall of the type likely to be found locally in the landscape. Alternatively, one could enclose the garden with a close thicket of pines, shrub roses or some other suitable plant.

In quite unspoilt surroundings, meadows of grass and wild flowers should be allowed to grow freely close to the house, avoiding closely-mown lawns. A single flowering forsythia, a *Kolkwitzia amabilis*, or a species rose like *Rosa hugonis* or *R.moyesii* would not be out of place, provided it was planted in the grass against the house – and indeed, such a flowering bush would remind one of people's need for beauty during the harsh, every-day life of a mountain region. But don't plant the bush in a bed of earth raked up all around it. This is the tell-tale sign of the town-dweller with his urban ideas, so out of place in the mountain environment.

62 A Balcony Garden

Many blocks of flats and apartments have large balconies, often south-facing, which can be transformed into a type of 'hanging garden'. The floors of the balconies have drains and are effectively insulated against water and dampness, so that plants can be watered without risk to the residents below! However, the load-bearing capacity of the balcony should be checked before setting up beds or large containers for trees such as those suggested shown in the illustration. However, ordinary-sized pots and window boxes should be perfectly satisfactory. Other smallish trees for balcony and roof gardens include laburnums and Japanese maples, while clematis and climbing roses do well if given enough room to root.

Plant containers and soil
Containers for plants should be as large and as spacious as poss-ible, and preferably be made of wood well impregnated with preservative (*not* creosote). They must have drainage holes. Ready-made containers are available in innumerable shapes and sizes. The soil in the containers should be rich and porous. It is better to buy John Innes potting compost than to use ordinary garden soil. If good soil can be obtained, it should be mixed with about 25% peat and a little gravel, plus a big handful of 2 parts bone meal and 1 part hoof and horn meal per bucketful. Before filling the boxes, a layer of broken flower pots or coarse gravel 5cm (2in) thick should be placed at the bottom of the container to provide sufficient drainage.

Looking after a roof garden
It is easier to grow trees and shrubs in a roof garden, whereas one must be content with just boxes of annuals and climbing plants on a smaller balcony. Trees and shrubs on a roof garden grow spectacularly provided they are kept well watered and given extra liquid fertilizer throughout the summer.

62   Window Boxes

The balcony is the town-dweller's miniature garden. Provided
it is of reasonable size and faces in the right direction with regard
to the sun, it can be a splendid garden where you can even sun-
bathe among flowers and greenery.

Plant containers for the balcony
A plant container for the balcony should be *at least* 20cm (8in)
deep and wide – and preferably about 25cm (10in) – and about
1m (3ft) long. Wooden boxes can easily be clumsy in appearance;
but there are plenty of plastic and asbestos-cement boxes. The
window boxes should always have 3–5 small holes in the base
and be given a thin drainage layer of broken flower pots before
filling them with soil. As for roof gardens, the soil should be rich
and porous and contain plenty of moisture-retaining peat.
Regular feeding is advisable since the constant watering which
is needed will also soon wash out the chemicals in the soil.

Planting window boxes
These days, most bedding-out plants are sold in plastic containers
or peat pots. The latter allow the roots to grow through, but
plastic pots must be carefully removed before planting. Be careful not to plant out too early as night frost can occur and nights
with temperatures only a few degrees above freezing can badly
damage many annuals. Do not begin planting out just because
the plants are in the shops; they are only there because of public
demand. In warmer latitudes, and especially in towns, the end
of late spring should be safest.

Plants in a window box should be planted closer together than
for the same flowers in a garden bed as they must appear abun-
dantly vigorous, and look as though they were about to overflow
the container. For a long box 1m (3ft) long, one should use 3–5
large plants and 6–8 smaller plants. If in doubt about the
arrangement, it is wise to use only one, or at the most two,
varieties with equal numbers of each. Some 4–6 hanging plants
should be placed in the foreground.

Besides the plants listed in Plate 63, the following can also
be recommended for a south-facing balcony: *Felicia amelloides*

the kingfisher daisy, *Gazania splendens*, bush sweet peas, *Matricaria eximia* and penstemons. On an east or west-facing balcony *Callistephus chinensis* or China asters, fuchsias, *Lobelia pumila*, *Mimulus luteus* the monkey flower and nasturtiums are suitable. Even on a north-facing balcony, many flowers can be grown, including French marigolds (tagetes), fuchsias, calceolarias, both hanging and edging lobelia, creeping jenny and begonias.

Looking after the plants
Plants in window-boxes can be tremendously vigorous as long as they are given water and extra fertilizer throughout the summer. In dry weather, water daily, and feed weekly with liquid fertilizer. It is important to dead-head daily, not only for appearance sake but also to avoid the formation of seed heads, which stops the plants producing any more flower buds.

Wind can be a problem for erect plants and just tying up with string is not satisfactory as the string may cut the plant to pieces. Something more secure is needed, such as stiff plastic mesh fixed to well-secured uprights. It also helps to place the window boxes on the floor of the balcony so that they are protected by the wall.

Window boxes throughout the year
Window boxes are not only usable in the summer, but throughout the year. In the early spring it can contain low spring bulbs such as botanical tulips, scillas, muscari and crocuses which have been planted in the autumn. These can be replaced with colourful spring flowers such as forget-me-not, pansies, wall-flowers, polyanthus and bachelors' buttons (double daisies); or, even better, these plants can be put in during autumn with the bulbs between them.

64 Pots, Boxes and Tubs

Now that bedding plants have become so expensive, many gardeners are not growing them extensively in beds but rather in pots, boxes and tubs. Placed on terraces or in patios, these provide focal points of colour even in gardens largely of shrubs.

The most attractive type of flowerpot is probably that of red clay, but for this purpose it should not be less than 50cm (20in) in diameter. Plant containers of cement, asbestos-cement and composition stone can also look attractive, especially after they have acquired some patina in the course of time. Wooden tubs are very attractive and could easily be made from old barrels cut in half with the staves cleaned and varnished and the metal bands painted to rust-preserve them.

Soil and nourishment

These plant containers require a rich, porous soil mixture just like that used for the roof and window box gardens. There should always be holes in the base of pots, boxes or tubs and before adding soil, a fairly deep drainage layer of coarse gravel or broken flower pots should be placed at the bottom of the container. If the containers stand on a warm, south-facing terrace, they should be watered every evening throughout the summer or during dry weather. Three or four times during the summer they will need a good feed of liquid fertilizer. As a rule, it is wise to empty clay pots and asbestos-cement boxes in winter. This will prevent damage following a severe frost, when the soil can expand and crack the containers.

Selection of plants

Generally speaking, the selection of plants is the same as for window boxes. When planting out into these containers, it is wise not to mix too many different types of flowers in the same vessel. Instead, attempt to form an attractive grouping with three or four main colours, as in Plate 64. Pleasant, peaceful effects can also be obtained by using only foliage plants such as hostas, periwinkle, ferns and variegated iries. In the right place, a Japanese bonsai tree could also look charming in an attractive pottery container.

ENGLISH AND LATIN NAMES OF PLANTS

The common English names of flowers and plants are given here with their taxanomic Latin names.

Abies nobilis   silver spruce
Acer palmatum   Japanese maple
Acer platanoides   Norway maple
Aesculus hippocastanum   horsechestnut
Agrostis alba   fiorin grass
Ailanthus altissima   tree of heaven
Allium schoenoprasum   chives
Amaryllis belladonna   belladonna lily
Anethum graveolens   dill
Aralia elata   Japanese angelica tree
Aristolochia durior   Dutchman's pipe
Artemisia absinthium   wormwood
Artemisia dracunculus   tarragon
Aruncus silvester   goat's-beard
Asarum europaeum   asarabacca
Asperula odorata   sweet woodruff
Aster novi-belgii   Michaelmas daisy
Astilbe arendsii   garden meadowsweet
Astrantia major   masterwort

Betula pendula   weeping birch
Briza maxima   greater quaking grass
Brunnera macrophylla   Siberian bugloss
Butomus umbellatus   flowering rush
Buxus sempervirens   box

Calendula   pot marigold
Calla palustris   bog arum
Callistephus chinensis   China asters
Calluna vulgaris   ling
Caltha palustris   marsh marigold
Cardamine amara   lady's smock
Carpinus betulus   hornbeam
Carum carvi   caraway
Cedrus atlantica   Atlas cedar
Centaurea cyanus   cornflower
Centranthus ruber   red valerian

Cercidiphyllum japonicum   Judas tree
Chaenomeles japonica   Japanese quince
Chamaecyparis obtusa   dwarf cypress
Chrysanthemum frutescens   marguerite
Chrysanthemum maximum   shasta daisy
Cimicifuga racemosa   black snake-root
Cornus alba   dogwood
Cornus mas   Cornelian cherry
Corydalis lutea   yellow fumitory
Corylus avellana   corkscrew hazel
Cotinus coggygria   smoke tree
Cupressocyparis laylandii   Leyland cypress
Cytisus praecox   bush broom

Dicentra spectabilis   bleeding heart

Elaeagnus commutata   silver berry
Enkianthus campanulatus   pagoda bush
Eremurus robustus   foxtail lily
Erica carnea   heather
Eryngium amethystinum   sea holly

Fagus sylvatica   copper (purple) beech
Felicia amelloides   kingfisher (blue) daisy
Festuca glauca   blue fescu grass
Festuca ovina   blue fescu
Foeniculum vulgare   fennel
Fritillaria imperialis   crown imperial

Galtonia candicans   summer hyacinth
Ginkgo bilboa   maidenhair tree

Hedera helix   ivy
Helianthus salicifolius   perennial willow-leafed sunflower

Hemerocallis   day lily
Hesperis matronalis   Dame's Violet
Hippophaë rhamnoides   sea buckthorn
Hordeum jubatum   squirrel-tail grass
Hosta fortunei   plantain lily
Hottonia palustris   water violet
Hydrocharis morsus-ranae   frogbit
Hypericum calycinum   rose of Sharon, St. John's wort
Hyssopus officinalis   hyssop

Iberis sempervirens   perennial candytuft
Iberis umbellata   annual candytuft
Ilex aquifolium   holly
Iris pseudacorus   yellow flag

Juglans regia   walnut
Juniperus communis   juniper
Juniperus media   Chinese juniper

Lagurus ovatus   hare's tail
Lamium galeobdolon variegatum yellow archangel
Lamium maculatum   variegated deadnettle
Laurus nobilis   bay
Lavandula officinalis   lavender
Lepidum sativum   cress
Levisticum officinale   lovage
Ligustrum vulgare   common privet
Lilium candidum   Madonna lily
Lilium regale   regal lily
Liriodendron tulipifera   tulip tree
Lonicera pileata   honeysuckle privet
Lonicera henryi   red and yellow honeysuckle
Lonicera tellmanniana   yellow honeysuckle
Lysimachia clethroides   white loosestrife
Lysimachia nummularia   creeping jenny

Mahonia aquifolium   Oregon grape
Matricaria chamomilla   camomile

Melissa officinalis   lemon balm
Mentha crispa   mint
Mentha piperita   mint
Mentha spicata   mint
Menyanthes trifoliata   bog bean
Metasequoia glyptostroboides   dawn redwood
Mimulus luteus   monkey flower
Miscanthus sacchariflorus   elephant grass
Musa ensete   ornamental banana
Myosotis scorpioides   marsh forget-me-not

Nasturtium officinale   watercress
Nigella damascena   love-in-the-mist

Oenothera   evening primrose
Origanum marjorana   marjoram

Paeonia lactiflora   peony
Paeonia officinalis   double peony
Papaver orientalis   oriental poppy
Petroselinum crispum   parsley
Picea brewerana   weeping spruce
Picea glauca   white spruce
Picea omorika   Serbian spruce
Picea pungens   blue spruce
Picea sitchensis   Sitka spruce
Pimpinella anisum   aniseed
Pinus contorta   beach pine
Pinus griffithii   Himalayan pine
Pinus mugo   dwarf pine
Pinus nigra   Austrian pine
Pinus sylvestris   Scots pine
Polygonatum multiflorum   Solomon's seal
Populus alba   white poplar
Populus canescens   grey poplar
Populus nigra   Lombardy poplar
Prunus cerasifera   purple plum
Prunus laurocerasus   cherry laurel
Pterocarya fraxinifolia   wing nut
Pyracantha coccinea   firethorn

Quercus borealis   red oak
Quercus robur   common oak

Ranunculus lingua   greater spearwort
Reseda odorata   mignonette
Rheum palmatum   rhubarb
Rhus typhina   sumach
Ribes alpinum   mountain currant
Robinia pseudoacacia   false acacia
Rosmarinus officinalis   rosemary
Rudbeckia hirta   gloriosa daisies
Rumex acetosa   sorrel
Ruta graveolens   rue

Sagittaria sagittifolia   arrowhead
Salix chrysocoma   weeping willow
Salix matsudana fortuosa   corkscrew
                                        willow
Salix purpurea   willow
Salvia officinalis   sage
Sambucus nigra   golden elder
Sanvitalia procumbens   creeping
                                        zinnia
Satureia hortensis   summer savory
Sciadopitys verticillata   umbrella pine
Sedum spectabile   ice plant
Sinarundinaria murielae   bamboo

Solidago   goldenrod
Stachys lanata   lamb's ears
Stratiotes aloides   water soldier
Symphoricarpos albus   snowberry
Symphoricarpos rivularis   snowberry
Syringa chinensis   Rouen lilac
Syringa vulgaris   lilac

Tagetes   marigold
Taxus baccata   yew
Thymus vulgaris   thyme
Tilia platyphylla   broad-leafed lime
Trollius hybridus   globe flower
Typha angustifolia   cat-tail

Ulmus glabra   wych elm

Vaccinium corymbosum   blueberry
Verbascum   muleins
Verbascum dympicum   greater mullein
Viburnum burkwoodii   snowball tree
Vinca minor   lesser periwinkle
Vitis vinifera   vine

Yucca filamentosa   Adam's needle

Zea mays   common maize